Heirs of The Great Migration

How the Past Became the Future

By James "Manny" Wright, PhD, MBA

DEDICATION

This book is dedicated to my beloved matriarchs: my grandmother, Dazell Omega Bumpers Wright and my mother, Lynda Darnell Wright Williams. Layla for her patience and grace and for giving me the three best things I never knew I needed—my three sons. In loving memory of Tracey McKnight (Cousin Tra Mack), Reese Wright (Cousin Ree), and Santosha Sears (Cousin Tash).

Contents

ACKNOWLEDGMENTS

This book manifests from faith, love, encouragement, and support from my loving and robust family. Specifically, my maternal grandparents who had 15 children, resulting in my many cousins. Childhood friends (remaining and departed), educators, mentors, and influencers who I met throughout life.

The City of Waterbury. Everyone I grew up with, those I observed, took life lessons from, showed me love, and broke bread with me—too many to name. My friends and relatives in Atlanta and throughout Georgia, Harlem, Brooklyn, and New Jersey. Gratitude to Jason Swain from the BX, and the Mitchell/Privott family.

All of the brothers who became my family while in Cairo, Egypt.

Editors and contributors who helped tie the book production include Gia'na Garel and a small trusted circle of friends and advisors in San Diego and Southern California. Contributors/advisers/sources of information include Malcolm X; Richard Wright; DuBois; Carter G. Woodson's *The Miseducation of The Negro*; Nathan McCall's *Makes Me Wanna Holler*; Ta-Nehisi Coates's *Between The World and Me*; James Baldwin's *Letter to My Nephew*; Claude Brown's *Manchild in the Promised Land*; Isabel

Wilkerson's *The Warmth of Other Suns*; these and others fueled and influenced this book.

Much appreciation to teachers/mentors/bosses such as Mrs. Shirly Norman; Mrs. Lillian Head; Mrs. Cheryl Savage and Wilby HS teachers. Former Michigan State University Professors Lynn Fendler and Muhammad Khalifa, my homie, mentor, and brother. Dr. Chris Dunbar, may you RIP.

A lifelong load of thanks to the inspiration received from my elder first cousins and first superheroes: Bo, Claudel (C-Dale), Tracey (Tra Mack), Stevie, Jake, Reese, Baron, and Derreck. The North End of Waterbury, and a special nod to the late, great Dr. Christopher Blake Love (C-Love). EB and Cousin Squirt for coining the term Dirty Water to more accurately describe the city of Waterbury—the home of the dopest MCs in CT. Will, Jug, Mas, and Jerz. Thanks to my growth experiences in ATL, Cairo, Michigan, and California, and the people there who inspired and showed me love. My brothers—DJ WIZdom Music, aka Scott, and his younger brother Mell from SC/Charlotte: Thanks for the beats, the music, inspiration, and friendship.

This book intends to encourage and inspire young Black boys and men as they navigate a matrix of anti-Blackness on their life journey in the US. This book also aims to encourage all those who love, care for, value, and are concerned about the plight and well-being of young Black men and boys in the US and throughout the diaspora.

FOREWORD

Heirs of the Great Migration: How the Past Became the Future, Professor James Wright captures personal accounts of the Great Migration in vivid detail. Building from Isabel Wilkerson's ground-breaking *The Warmth of Other Suns*, Wright interweaves stories of faith, family, freedom, determination, and vision, recounting a family's long legacy of resistance—from overcoming enslavement to his grandparents and mother fleeing the Jim Crow South and the brutal tyranny of debt-peonage and sharecropping in rural North Carolina, and to new forms of racism and anti-Blackness in the North. With his experiences and the generations before and after, Wright weaves a story of history, pain, trauma, and truth. Wright draws from Wilkerson to tell stories of suffering and overcoming as part of the Great Migration that connects the past, present, and future. Wright extends migration stories by including preceding generations' inheritance—an inventory of his ancestors' hopes and aspirations for their future offspring.

I had the privilege of watching this story unfold over a decade. Starting with a bond and a brotherhood that began in Cairo, Egypt, I witnessed Wright embody both the present and the past. True to whom I came to know, he continues in relentless pursuit of an approachable scholarly work that counteracts narratives that frame and define Black life in deficit lights, in a vacuum, and without historical context. Wright masterfully embraces his troubled past as a young boy raised by street codes and inspired by individuals involved with every aspect of street life. Wright brightens the dim lights in the streets by focusing on the humanity of the characters in the book and offers another layer of consideration underlying their reality. Staring trauma in the face and recognizing that his failures and triumphs are much bigger than himself, *Heirs of the Great Migration* is a collection of lessons to help generations of Black boys growing up in an anti-Black world see the fullness of possibilities without ignoring or underselling the white supremacy structured against them. These structures and systems of white supremacy are historicized and contextualized to help understand what our ancestors endured and how they conducted themselves and overcame. They were survivors. Thus, Wright focuses on survival tactics as a guide from the past and a blueprint for the future.

Heirs of the Great Migration is a must-read for teachers and educational leaders who wish to move closer to understanding and humanizing the experiences, identities, and ways of knowing of Black as well as similarly racially minoritized students. This book is essential reading for those raising and caring for Black boys and men, educators, teachers, and educational leaders who wish to become better informed of the contexts of oppression that our Black and other minoritized students face: de-industrialism, illicit drug encroachment, mass incarceration, and federally sponsored and funded destruction of Black communities. For culturally responsive school leaders, it is necessary to understand the contexts and histories of our students and communities, past and present, to see a future where Black life can thrive outside structures that continue to dehumanize, brutalize, and disenfranchise. Most importantly, this book is for generations of Black boys becoming men, who will now have another story of triumph they can see themselves in and lean on and witness an example of Black manhood to follow.

Wright draws on ancestral knowledge, enacting self-reflection, and self-determination, vulnerably connecting with the darker sides of his past, the enlightenment of his spiritual journey, and the ways deep family bonds shaped him. Wright takes great pride in stepping into the shoes of his ancestors. Connecting their spaces with his own and those of his sons will continue to tread spaces that are not only the physical locations depicted but also the social and historical contexts associated with communities bonded by faith and love.

Emulating a character arc of his own, including the defiant life and tragic death of his mother, Lynda, and of many dear friends and cousins, Wright forges a path of healing by reflecting on the twists and turns of his life and the ways that ancestral power has ultimately guided him. Told in a narrative, autobiographical voice, Wright lays bare the joys and sufferings of Blackamerican life, the strength from his family, community, and ancestral knowledge that grounds his life, fatherhood, and scholarship. Generations of Black defiance and the continuous stream of opposition to Black progress are unearthed in this raw and inspiring oral history.

Dr. Muhammad Khalifa

Professor Ohio State University

Founder of the Culturally Responsive School Leadership Institute

INTRODUCTION

I was leaving the South
To fling myself into the unknown . . .
I was taking a part of the South
To transplant in alien soil,
To see if it could grow differently,
If it could drink of new and cool rains,
Blend in strange winds,
Respond to the warmth of other suns
And, perhaps, to bloom.
– Richard Wright

They did not ask to be accepted but declared themselves the
Americans that perhaps few others recognized but that they had
always been deep within their hearts.
– Wilkerson, 2010, p. 538, referring to the Southern migrants'
escape from a land of enforced segregation

This book is inspired by Isabel Wilkerson's groundbreaking national
bestseller, *The Warmth of Other Suns: The Epic Story of America's Great
Migration*. It is a personal account of my family's migration from the South
told from my perspective and lived experiences as a Blackamerican man in
the United States of America. As the offspring of those *legally* denied
fundamental human rights. Such as the right to nurture and raise their
families with dignity. Rights denied based on three centuries of enslavement

and a century of Jim Crow (legalized segregation). However, our ancestors managed to survive this traumatic legacy.

Additionally, our ancestors left us with survival tools and a meticulous understanding of their enslavers, who capitalized from a matrix of contrived laws designed to misappropriate our ancestors' physical labor and intellectual property. Subsequently, these practices led to a transfer of wealth, which became a pillar of the US empire and the centerpiece of the generational wealth accrued by the institutions of enslavement. In other words, the human trafficking network known as US chattel slavery financed the US empire. Enslavement in the US thrived due to an assemblage of financiers and banking systems, transportation and insurance networks, and other industries that helped it flourish. And lastly, those who inherited the spoils of this human trafficking criminal network complete this transfer of wealth.

The Civil Rights Movement struggle of the 1960s, waged by Blacks and other co-conspirators, offered Black people a semblance of a long-overdue compensation for their Human Rights violations in the US. In 400-plus years of US history, the post-1964 Civil Rights Era (Generation X, 1964–1981) Blacks were indeed the first of their lineage born with all of the rights afforded by the US Constitution. I was born in the post-1964 Civil Rights Era. In other words, I am among the first generations of Blackamericans born with *all* the rights afforded by the Constitution. Consequently, my family members born before 1964 were born during an era wherein the US Constitution did not fully apply to Blacks in the US, such as the Jim Crow laws of segregation. This includes my mother who was born in 1954, and her mother in 1923.

Put another way, the same instruments used to build the modern world's most formidable super-power were used to enslave, dehumanize, and oppress our ancestors—two sides of the same coin: two inseparable realities. I am a descendant of survivors of incomprehensible trauma whose sons and daughters abandoned the Jim Crow South, debt-peonage, and sharecropping, in search of opportunities afforded by the Industrial Revolution in the North. Those who, in turn, unintentionally and unknowingly left behind for their progeny (my generation) deindustrialization and mass incarceration. As factories closed and offshored, tons of illicit drugs and narcotics filled the gaps. Simultaneously, intricate systems of high-level and powerful individuals carved out sophisticated logistical networks that flooded the most divested Black and Brown communities with cocaine and crack from coast to coast: from the largest cities to the relatively obscure ones such as the one where I was raised, Waterbury, Connecticut. Consequently, a Thirteenth Amendment loophole, deindustrialization, the crack cocaine and subsequent mass incarceration epidemics, and my experience growing up highlight and inspire the stories told in this book. I tell these stories as the great-great-grandson and grandson of former sharecroppers in the Jim Crow South who resisted and escaped in search of better opportunities for themselves and their future generations.

3

However, I tell these stories from the status and sociopolitical position my Jim Crow migrant forefathers only envisioned, hoped, and prayed for. Had they been told that someone from their future generations would hold academic degrees such as an MBA and a PhD, I'm sure they would have thought their faith, toil, aspirations, and sacrifices were worthwhile. On the surface, this may be true. As a college professor, my colleagues and peers are among the brightest minds nationally and abroad. I write syllabi, teach classes, give lectures, and publish in academic journals. But in this book, I return to my roots and reveal experiences that shaped and brought me to this point. I inherited my ancestors' blueprint and will to survive—a wealth that does not register economically. This book outlines my application of that blueprint. It is not the story of all Blackamericans, but I know it is a prominent version and one rarely told.

My journey was filled with every trap known to ensnare Black people in the US, especially Black men. These traps include broken K-12 schools, school-to-prison pipelines, widespread police brutality, harassment, petty arrests, drug trafficking, and mass incarceration, all of which I know very well. These structural and systemic realities are often mistaken as excuses for the predicament many Blackamericans find themselves in. I was raised fully aware that life is full of choices, and I take responsibility for mine. However, the choices that I inherited are contextualized by historical structures, systems, hardships, and obstacles set in place long before me. Knee-jerk meritocracy comments like "tighten your bootstraps" and "work hard" are disingenuous and ahistorical tropes and only serve those who benefit from and are favored by the systems put in place long ago.

CHAPTER ONE
The Strange Fruit of Migration

I was hoping I would be able to live as a man and express myself in
a manly way without the fear of getting lynched at night.
– Wilkerson, 2010, p. 229, quoting George Starling, the third main
character of this book, who fled Florida for New York after his
attempts to get higher pay for Black orange-pickers nearly cost him
his life

My great-grandfather, John Bumpers, aka Sonny-Man, left Franklin
County's City of Louisburg in North Carolina around 1940. He moved to
New York City's borough of Manhattan, where he lived at 364 West 119th
Street in Harlem. He was a New York City bus driver until he died on June
21, 1961, at 55.

While it took only a few words to sum up his life and death, he
planted seeds for what would eventually become a large family. Yet
regardless of how far away he moved to live out his life, he returned to his
roots for his burial. My grandmother, Dazell Omega Bumpers Wright, his
oldest child, was responsible for his burial among his family at Old Liberty
Cemetery on June 27, 1961, in Louisburg, North Carolina.

Growing up, elders in our family often indicated how much I
resembled Sonny-Man, which led to my nickname "Manny." And while I

might have resembled one before me, I had to come of age in a land foreign to my ancestors and those before me.

In 2020, as I began outlining this book, the US faced a perfect storm. Popular buzzwords such as *elections, mass incarceration, pandemic, George Floyd, racial protests, CRT, anti-Blackness, and white supremacy* were common. By now, I had a 40-plus-year view as a Black man both inside this country and from living abroad.

While compiling my life history, I noticed what many Blackamericans already knew; the rest of the world was now learning. The US had either fallen apart, was falling apart, or merely revealed its moral, sociopolitical, and cultural bankruptcy despite its popular claims as the world's wealthiest country.

Growing up, I watched *things* once valued deteriorate around me, like the hopes and dreams that drove my family out of the Jim Crow South into the North. The bustling factories that brought my family to Waterbury became eye sores that blighted the city as I was growing up. As a result, many prominent Black communities and families declined. Growing up, loving Black families were the glue that held Black communities together. These loving communities and families raised me and shaped the man I am today.

Holding on to Hope

In October 2017, my mother's remission changed what had been holding steady. Pancreatic cancer came back. I had been in the thick of a rigorous doctoral program at Michigan State University. Still, I flew to Raleigh,

North Carolina, to hear my mom's oncologist inform us that there was nothing more that he could do. He predicted that she had about 6 to 9 months left to live. My mom and I left the doctor's office and went to her home in Raleigh, where she had retired just four years prior after working 40-plus years for the State of Connecticut as an accountant. She told me all of her last wishes and precisely what she wanted. She wanted to go on a cruise and visit the newly minted National Museum of African American History and Culture in Washington, DC. Mom asked to be buried in purple and that all her family members wear that color in solidarity.

With Thanksgiving just one month away, she wanted a big celebration dinner speculating that it might be her last. Mom valued holidays and gatherings and loved cooking for large groups of family and friends, who'd come together to laugh and reminisce. We planned what was possibly her last big family dinner at a hotel in Raleigh, and family from across North Carolina and as far as Connecticut came.

My mother was unapologetic in her Blackness; she loved Black people, Black culture, and the Black family. And she imparted many of these values and wisdom in raising me. My mom would make plans without telling anyone, which sometimes felt spontaneous. For example, after retirement in 2014, she moved back to her birthplace in North Carolina from my native city of Waterbury, Connecticut. Almost no one saw this coming, although she often talked about going "back home" when I was growing up. The timing proved good because the following year, in May of 2015, she was diagnosed with cancer. It was a tough time because her mother, my beloved grandmother, Dazell Omega Bumpers Wright, who was also living in North Carolina, passed a few months later, on September 12, 2015.

Since my mom was in Raleigh, the family from Waterbury would have to come down to join the majority of the family already there for our Thanksgiving family gathering. A planning committee comprised of me, my cousin, Tracey McKnight (known affectionally as Cousin Mack, or Tra Mack), and my youngest aunt, Naomi (Aunt Nay). Although Tra Mack was a part of the initial conversations about food, hotel reservations, booking a venue, etc., he suddenly went silent, and I didn't know why.

Tra Mack is my first cousin and one of my mom's favorite nephews. His absence from our planning event was odd and indicated that something was wrong; even worse, he didn't make it to the dinner. Months later, I got word he had some health issues, but nothing specific.

In October 2018, 12 months after my mom's oncologist informed us that she had 6 to 9 months remaining, a lot had transpired. I had completed my doctoral studies at Michigan State University, was recently hired as a tenure-track or full-time professor, and relocated to Southern California. Also, in October 2018, my Cousin Baron got married and had his wedding in Waterbury, Connecticut, and I was one of his groomsmen. My mother was hanging in strong and was determined to join us all at the wedding in Connecticut.

I had not returned to Connecticut since I left for graduate school at Michigan State in 2013. One week before leaving California for Connecticut for Baron's wedding, my mother called me about the wedding details. "Hey,

Tracey (Tra Mack) said that you were coming to Connecticut and that you were staying with him," she said.

"Yeah, I'm flying back for the wedding, but I didn't talk to him about staying with him. But I'll do that if he wants me to."

"Yeah, that'll probably make him happy."

"Alright, say no more; I'll fly in, get a rental car, and go to his house from the airport."

I flew into Bradley International Airport, north of Hartford, and drove my rental car 45 minutes south into Waterbury. Traveling home is always bitter-sweet. Being home again was not about the city's remnants of decaying factories and old "up-from-the-South" ancestral dreams dying there among them. It wasn't about the wild street life I'd known so well and narrowly escaped. It was about the family that waited there to welcome me no matter where I'd been or what I'd been up to. It was always love waiting, whether coming home from a stint in prison or as a PhD and professor.

I plugged in my Cousin Tra Mack's address and started my journey. Tra was more than my big cousin; he was a big brother, a childhood hero, friend, guide, and mentor during the most pivotal years of my life. He was all of that, and though he'd gone silent over the past year, I was eager to see him after not seeing him in over five years since I left Connecticut in 2013. I'd been in California for approximately 9 or 10 months after nearly five years in Michigan. Seeing my family, and especially Tra Mack, was a reunion long overdue.

Tra Mack: My First Black Superhero and Cousin

For as long as I could remember, Tra Mack was muscular. He had broad shoulders, a wide chest, and a back like he'd been working out all his life. Tra Mack's physique, personality, and aura made him a larger-than-life figure.

According to the GPS, I finally arrived. I grabbed my bags from the rental car, walked up the steps to the door, and rang the doorbell. I was shocked when Tra opened the door. It took a few seconds to comprehend who was in front of me and how this happened. Tra was small.

The smallest version of Tra that I could ever recall. I was standing in front of a new smaller version of the larger-than-life individual who I grew up admiring and mimicking. I had to compose myself quickly as I quickly realized Tra was dying. Yes, I had heard he was privately struggling with his health, but I didn't anticipate the extent and how this might look. Although I crumbled on the inside, I kept it together, I think—I hope— enough so he could see I was being strong for him as he invited me into his home. The year prior, 2017, Tra Mack had been diagnosed with cancer and fought it privately.

Tra was strong and private and never wanted to appear weak or vulnerable. When the doctors found cancer, it had already metastasized.

I embraced him and walked inside the house like it was old times. It was basketball season, and the NBA was on. We stayed up late talking about teams and players, music, family updates, and catching up in general. It could almost be mistaken for "just like the old days," except it was apparent he was in a lot of pain. He reached for a tube of cream on the table nearby and asked if I could rub it into his back; I was happy to help. I'd never seen my cousin this vulnerable. Out of all the men in my family—and there were many alphas, kingly characters—Tra Mack was the one who was most admired and respected. I was seven years younger than Tra, I looked up to him more than anybody else in my family, and I was proud to be his little cousin.

When I was 14, he was 21, and even at that young age, he seemed to me to be an invincible titan who was one of the livest guys in the city. Everybody respected or feared him because he was not someone to play with. But fast forward to the present and me sitting behind him rubbing pain relief cream into his back until he told me he was "good." We stayed up all night reminiscing. I was tired from coast-to-coast travel, but it didn't matter. I was cool chilling with my big cousin, watching NBA highlights, and getting caught up.

The next day was my Cousin Baron's wedding rehearsal, and afterward, the wedding party gathered at a local town favorite pizza spot in Waterbury.

Tra Mack called me while I was there and said, "Come get me." This request was significant because he was a private person, and many family and friends didn't know that he was sick, and those who did were unaware of the extent. By then, I understood why he hadn't shown up or returned my calls during my mom's Thanksgiving planning and get-together the year before.

11

After his call, I announced to the wedding party, "I'll be back, I'm going to get Tra!" He hadn't been out in public much during these times because he was visibly vulnerable and his health had declined. He understood he was the source of strength for many of us.

Tra calling me to come and bring him to the pizza spot was a statement. I think Tra decided to make peace with his condition and entrusted me to take him out publicly. I picked him up and brought him back among many of his loved ones. We arrived, and Tra Mack walked in with a cane in one hand and his other arm wrapped around mine as I held him up from underneath his shoulder. It was the first time my Cousin Baron, the groom, had seen Cousin Tra since he had been diagnosed with cancer. I watched Baron's facial expression transform from joy to devastation, much like mine when I had arrived at Tra's house the night before. I saw some of the strongest men, relatives, and others who were a part of the wedding party emotionally implode like pillars holding up a temple at the sight of Tra's physical condition.

Tra sat down next to my mom, who had flown up from North Carolina, visiting for the first time since she was diagnosed with cancer, and since her retirement from the State of Connecticut four years prior in 2014. Despite her illness, dire condition, and rarely feeling well, she was determined to not miss her nephew Baron's wedding. I sensed that Tra had accepted the inevitable, and yet he embraced the moment and let everybody love on him.

After the initial shock, things got normal: people telling jokes, talking, and laughing loudly. It was a good night. After a couple of hours, I took Tra Mack home to rest as the focus re-shifted to the wedding the next day. We still managed to stay up all night again, kicking it, watching more basketball, and talking about music. I was surprised to hear his favorite artists because we hadn't talked like that in years. Like me, Jay-Z was his favorite, but Nas, Jadakiss, and Lox were in heavy rotation also. But from the newer generation, we shared similar favorites like Kendrick Lamar, Nipsey Hussle, J. Cole, and Rhapsody (the last two interestingly enough with roots in North Carolina, like us), none of which surprised me. We always had similar music tastes, but he was older, so it was interesting to hear him talking about the younger artists.

This night's conversation went beyond our childhood and deeper into the essence of our dying hometown, marked by dilapidated factories and warehouses, and how we got here in the first place. These conversations planted seeds of memory and inquiry rooted in our forefathers' migration from the Deep South into urban neighborhoods and streets where so many lives had withered away prematurely.

Like most of my male cousins in Waterbury, Tra Mack had done a stint in prison, and so did I. We knew a lot about street life. Although I barely escaped the snares of the streets, I retained many valuable lessons and principles, which are rooted in my historical memory and embedded in my DNA. No matter what one thinks about Blackamerican street life, it is a part of Blackamerican culture and history. Street life has carved a pivotal lane in every arena of American popular culture. It influenced every musical genre in the US, and its influence is also evident in movies, marketing, and advertisement.

Dirty Water: Deindustrialization and Street Life

Street life became a means of survival, which saved lives and fed many otherwise legally, structurally, and systemically locked out of white institutions. Ingenious Blackamericans found ways. And yes, the destruction that street life caused is not trivial nor insignificant, but that is not its only contribution. It is a mere fraction and a byproduct of the violence and destruction caused by white supremacy.

The legal and structural systems of violence and oppression at the behest of Eurocentric domination in the US, including genocide and native land theft, the kidnapping and enslavement of Black people and their forced labor, are the foundations for the current global economic and sociopolitical order. Blackamerican street life was and is a response to white supremacy—an essentially racialized global order of dominance and oppression.

Once an industrial force, Waterbury tolerated Black migrants pursuing manufacturing jobs and opportunities. Waterbury, also known as The Brass City, was pivotal for its brass production and other supplies that fueled the war machine in the early to mid-twentieth century. It was the place to be if you were a manufacturer. Our ancestors sought the promises of stability and upward mobility afforded by the industrial revolution. Subsequently, those jobs that lured our grandparents and elders dried up.

14

Tra Mack and I came of age during deindustrialization, as an entire industry and its infrastructure was gutted from the city and offshored. Once proud symbols of prosperity and hope, today, the factories in Waterbury are relics of an abandoned wasteland. Huge factory buildings stretching miles across city blocks were chained and locked up all my life. As symbols of hopelessness, these blighted factories were the skyscrapers and backdrop of the neighborhoods where we were raised. I never got to see Waterbury at its peak with my own eyes. Instead, my generation constantly asked flippantly, "Y'all left North Carolina to come here for *this*? Why?" We couldn't understand how or why Waterbury became a new center and a draw for Jim Crow migrants because all we saw was the plummet and wreckage. Nevertheless, our tribe managed to hold it together for a couple of decades after deindustrialization, even as the city was falling apart around us. But that which was holding us together was beginning to whither as well.

During my high school years, deindustrialization was complete. Waterbury was a source of heartache and embarrassment for the State of Connecticut. Political corruption, graft, scandals among elected officials and city elites, coupled with politically and economically divested Black and Brown neighborhoods flooded with drugs like crack cocaine, failed/broken school systems, and mass incarceration, is the most accurate description of my youth coming of age in the 1990s. Waterbury became known as the Dirty-Water by local hip hop artists. The term was used to describe the city's rampant political corruption, which led to federal investigations and convictions of rank-and-file city leaders and elected officials.

As we fast forward to 2018, reminiscing with Tra Mack and my bittersweet return home collided. As Baron's wedding signified new additions to our family, other pieces were being removed. These realizations emerged as I reached a pinnacle in my life, having survived all that I had to attain a doctorate and work in a dream profession. I realized that growing up was a juxtaposition of a dying city and being nurtured by some of the most loving and caring individuals I ever would come to know. I realized that I witnessed the city's death as I sat in the presence of two of the most nurturing people of my childhood, both taking what would soon be their last breaths.

These deaths carried multiple meanings. For example, when I was a child, it was common to find pear and apple trees and grapevines throughout the city. But if Tra Mack and I had decided to revisit the places where we knew fruit grew as kids, we would not find any. As we got older, it seemed as though the soil stopped providing fruit-bearing trees.

We saw first-hand the center of that city decay—industry, production, and potential—as some of its brightest minds relocated. That's not to say the people who stayed didn't have ambition, but there was an exodus of many of the best—ironically back to the South, the same Jim Crow cities and states that terrorized their ancestors. Some went to the Carolinas (e.g., Raleigh, Charlotte), but mostly Atlanta, where many Waterburians birthed and raised kids and grandkids. The collective of Waterburians now living in Atlanta is so large that they have an annual gathering called The Southern Side of Waterbury, held in Atlanta at Piedmont Park.

By 2018, the mass migration from Waterbury made the city appear as though a full-scale closure of what the city was and what it could have been had come to pass. The dialogue with Tra Mack that night helped me reflect on how I grew up loving and admiring my city because it raised me and taught me many valuable lessons.

It was painful to see and know someone central to my evolution as a young man, my Cousin Tra Mack, was also dying in Waterbury. My biological father was murdered when I was young; ironically, he had been born and raised in Harlem, where he was shot and killed. I had uncles, several much older male cousins, and a stepfather, but the male who I looked to more than anybody was Tra Mack.

On October 19, 2018, at the pizza lounge, with Tra sitting beside my mom, the unmistakable realization that I was losing them heightened juxtaposing feelings of joy and pain. The joy of what I overcame and accomplished and the new life opportunities in California was curtailed by the sudden and painful awareness of the death of the people and places that nurtured, inspired, and raised me.

On November 13, three weeks after we left Waterbury, my Cousin Tra Mack passed away. Tra and my mom established a bond based on their battle with cancer and the torment of cancer treatments. Tra's loss was devastating for us all, including my aunt—his mother, his three brothers, two sisters, his daughter, many nieces, nephews, cousins, and so many who loved him.

On May 30, 2019, about six months later, another devastating blow landed. This one was more impactful than the prior. The conduit that brought me here, my beloved mom, passed away. Two soul-shaking deaths, but not before we, she, Tra, and I were able to reunite one last time in Waterbury—the place where our relationship began—just as I was beginning a rebirth, a new life journey in California.

The wedding in October 2018 marked the first time I was in the city of Waterbury as a professor. I graduated from Michigan State University in December of 2017 with a PhD in Educational Leadership and K-12 Administration, and shortly after, I landed a faculty position in Southern California. I had evolved from the old me, widely known for wilding out and running the streets and headed towards either an early grave or a life of imprisonment.

But there's a notable gap between my years running the streets and my doctoral studies. This gap includes a short time at an HBCU in Virginia followed by relocation to Atlanta, where, against my will, I became a prisoner of the Georgia Department of Corrections. Prison in Georgia nonetheless led me on a spiritual quest that landed me in Egypt, where I reengaged with education and learning.

My new pathways and opportunities would have looked impossible based on my choices as a youth. It was ironic to have accomplished so much of what those two people, Tra Mack and Mom, inspired in me and have almost no time to share the achievement with them. Nevertheless, we were reunited in Connecticut at my Cousin Baron's wedding, a full circle.

The wedding in Connecticut would be the last time my mother and I would ever be together there, and when she returned to her roots, she didn't leave again. In Old Liberty Cemetery, she was buried where Sonny-Man, her grandfather, her mother, Dazell Omega Bumpers Wright, and others of our bloodline rest. There they all lie at the vast roots of a family tree so strong it, directly and indirectly, helped grow a boy into a man, despite unimaginable and unfathomable trauma and obstacles.

CHAPTER TWO
Navigating Dirty Water

She had lived the hardest life, been given the least education, seen
the worst the South could hurl at her people, and did not let it
break her . . . She was surrounded by the clipped speech of the
North, the crime on the streets, the flight of the white people from
her neighborhood, but it was as if she were immune to it all. She
took the best of what she saw in the North and the South and
interwove them in the way she saw fit . . .
– Wilkerson, 2010, p. 532, describing Ida Mae Gladney whose
stories Ms. Wilkerson tells

I was born in Waterbury, Connecticut, on January 25, 1973, at Waterbury
Hospital, adding to a legacy of Jim Crow migrants settling on the East
Coast and as far north as Buffalo, New York. I graduated from Wilby High
School in 1992. That same year, *Money Magazine* released findings from a
report ranking the 300 largest metropolitan cities in the country. Also in
1992, using various living standards such as crime, economics, and
education, *Money* ranked the city of Waterbury No. 300 out of 300 for the
second consecutive year.

In a 1992 *New York Times* article, "Wounded Waterbury: No Place
to Go but Up," reflecting on the back-to-back years of embarrassment for
the city, Bill Ryan wrote, "There lies Waterbury, perched up and down
some hills in (south) western Connecticut, still known as the Brass City

though the big brass companies have all passed away, a community down on its luck that obviously could use a bit of encouragement."

I often contemplate, what happened to Waterbury?

How did I end up growing up in the worst-ranked metropolitan city in the country, in one of its worst neighborhoods, in one of the worst high schools in a notoriously underperforming/failing Waterbury Public School District? Friends and family in our neighborhoods could barely escape the rampant lure of drug use and the surging market that addiction and recreational use sparked inWaterbury and the surrounding suburban towns. Despite the environment that I inherited, I was inspired to get out somehow and make a name for myself. With almost no connections outside of Waterbury, I had no clue how. But I was determined.

Tra inspired reflections that night from the current version of myself. The one who, decades prior, was determined to leave and suffered various setbacks and obstacles that led to the present—the post-Waterbury version of myself whose scars, trauma, and turmoil are barely covered. I had been many versions of a young man. I was a standout, all-state point guard high school basketball player, a petty local drug dealer, a prison inmate, and an ambitious musician/music mogul who made an impression on a childhood hero, Chuck D of Public Enemy. Multiple versions of myself culminated in the miracle of making it to full manhood and out of the clutches of a dying city. I often wondered what my elders thought I would become based on my environment and the options it offered? By 2018, I had become a university professor; I am confident this was an implausible prediction. I have the ability, expertise, training, insight, lived experience, and platform to speak with integrity against a school system that, unbeknownst to us then, was designed to disengage children from our communities.

My ancestors were ambitious dreamers, which motivated their brave journey from Jim Crow's offer of next-to-nothing to the promise and potential in the North closer-to-something. Family members who knew me as a young adolescent and the man I became were undoubtedly proud. Mom and Tra not only saw the beginning, the doctorate, and the university professorship, but they also witnessed my falls which may have seemed difficult to bounce back from. Admittedly, I rarely take inventory of my accomplishments; I just set goals and power through. But the sense of achievement was made tangible, seeing and knowing how proud they were. Tra and my mom understood what it took and what I had gone through to get to that point.

Other family members and elders, like my great-grandfather and look alike, Sonny-Man, simply kicked the foundation off and exited early. I never met him—his life ended at the age of 55, when my mother was just seven years old—and despite not living out any long-term ambitions he might have had, the seeds he planted still branched up and out into my cousins and me. Our *success* is his because, in the North, his bloodline found tools to survive traps similar to those he had often sought refuge from in the Jim Crow South.

Sharecropping: "Working" for Jim Crow

My great-grandparents' marriage certificate shows that in 1922, Sonny-Man—John Bumpers—married Lillie Bell Debnam. Their firstborn, Dazell Bumpers, my grandmother, arrived one year later on February 2, 1923. Families back then came fast and large—a commodity for white plantation owners and their sharecropper progeny in the South. A global, industrial revolution and a race for economic supremacy by Western nations offered families such as ours a choice to continue relying on white people's evasive goodwill and sharecrop—or abandon it all for fresh starts and join the manufacturing revolution up north and throughout the West. By the 1940s, Sonny-Man chose the latter and moved to Harlem.

His line spread out with 4 children, 3 boys and 1 daughter, by my great-grandmother, Lillie Bell Debnam. It further spread into an additional daughter in another relationship—a fact only later disclosed to our side of the family through tragedy. Sonny-Man and Lillie's oldest child, Dazell, my grandma. Then Johnny Leamon Bumpers (Bubba, who died as a young boy), then Uncle RB—Richard Bumpers (who served in the military and returned from World War II "shell-shocked" with undiagnosed PTSD). My grandmother's youngest sibling, great-Uncle Otis Bumpers moved to Buffalo and became one of the city's first Black police officers, but he also died young, yet his children and grandchildren remain there. In other words, the men, my grandmother's father and three brothers all died young but old enough to continue growing the family tree.

Essentially, my great-grandad and his three sons all died relatively young. Yet, my beloved grandmother, the oldest child, lived to see 92 years of age when she died in September 2015. My grandmother, Dazell Bumpers Wright, was affectionately referred to as muh, short for mother. Everyone called her muh, her children, her grandchildren and great-grandchildren, and most of our friends. Muh had 13 children born in Jim Crow Franklin County, North Carolina. My mom, Lynda, was the eighth child, born in 1954 on the Brooks Young farm. As a family of sharecroppers, my mother's earliest memories were working on the farm as young as age four, carrying bails of tobacco from the field into the barn. I inquired about this "work" one day at her home outside of Raleigh about one year before she passed away; "It was hard work," is how she described it.

Fleeing Jim Crow: A Leap of Faith North

In 1963, muh and her seven youngest children, all girls, including my nine-year-old mother, moved to Connecticut following the trail of Sonny-Man, who started the trek north in 1940. My grandfather, my mother's father, George Oliver Wright, moved to the Brownsville section of Brooklyn, New York, in the 1950s. Southern Connecticut is a bedroom community to New York City. When it thrived in its heyday, it beckoned just as loudly as the Big Apple for hardworking families and progressive, hopeful Southerners looking for a new start and a brighter future.

The area that my mother, maternal grandmother, and my aunts settled in was by any measure ruggedly blue-collared and not for the faint-hearted. It was city life drastically different from their rural North Carolina

24

roots. But was the life that the Brass City, Waterbury, Connecticut offered my elders as rough as the hardships and insults in the Jim Crow South? How much trauma, internalized frustration at the disrespect and undignified treatment did they harbor inside? How much drive did they possess to risk everything they knew to escape it? Once they did, were these Northern hardships the lesser of two evils? To be living on the edge of violence and premature death, hustling for extra dollars, or toiling away for even less somewhere south? Was the harsh environments in the North reflections from or reactions to genetically inherited trauma, tensions, and frustrations manifesting on the streets up north? Granted, those who chose to escape Jim Crow were less restrained and had more choices, but it still wasn't easy.

In some ways, the North offered more choices for who they could be and how their future could look. Sharecroppers doing the "hard work" on a farm where farmers paid profits as peonage was a dehumanizing dead end. Each lineage received a dice roll, and theoretically, the odds increase for large families. But my big family seemed to be ensnared by traps they could not see, perceive, or comprehend. These traps were the hallmark of white supremacy with historical roots. Essentially traps designed to maintain leverage and power. The roadblocks that inhibited our ancestors in the Jim Crow South, albeit less explicit, had the same inhibiting effect on us, the children of the first generations of Jim Crow migrants who moved north. In Waterbury, this was indicative of divested communities, failed schools, neighborhoods ravaged by a crack cocaine epidemic, and a police culture patrolling our neighborhoods as occupied territory, targeting and undermining our strongest and brightest men and women.

In the South, it was not uncommon for plantation owners and their sharecropper offspring to have small families, one or two children, contrasting Black families who might have 10 or 12. For example, my grandparents and my mom's 12 siblings did all the labor and farming. I was told of these realities by mom and two of my oldest aunts, who had all been born in the 1940s and worked the Brooks Young farm as young as 4- and 5-year-olds until they were teens. Additional insight was conveyed to me by my Cousin Truman Cooke, who still lives in North Carolina and recalls many branches of our family tree. Truman, born in 1947, is one of our family's oral historians. Truman's mother, Serena Debnam, and my maternal, great grandmother, Lillie Bell Debnam Bumpers were sisters. Truman explained to me that our family's source of survival was sharecropping their labor. I asked him, "How did enslavement end, but our family continued living as though still enslaved?" He replied, "After freedom, a lot of Black folks bought land, but the government had a system for them to borrow money that seemed unlimited, more than can be paid back. Then they would foreclose. So many of our ancestors owned land, but banks and investors over-loaned to Black landowners who managed to take it (the land) right back."

My great-great-grandfather, Sonny-Man's dad, James (Jim) Bumpers (1872–1950), who was born just after slavery ended, lost his land bought after Reconstruction just that way. Truman continued, "He had his land when I was a child, a farm behind Flat Rock Church, there near another family—the Smiths who lost theirs the same way."

What did being landless have to offer the men in my family that Harlem, Brooklyn, Waterbury, and Buffalo didn't? That Jim Crow legal system was a slow noose, and they knew it. The landless man who stayed on property they once owned, had it swindled away by white folks who wouldn't allow them to repurchase any of it. They only allowed them to sharecrop it for sustenance.

Truman recalled, "Oh, they'd sell you a few acres for a dollar or two—which was a lot of money then—to build you a house on but nothing much more than that. So you farmed for them under a percentage-based system they had in place. One great-uncle was fortunate to get to farm for the ½ profit system where whatever he made from the harvest; he kept half. But mostly, it was ¼ or 25% of your labor as profit, and your supplies and food and things had to be deducted from what you earned. Then you had to take care of family in the off-season with no crops producing, so they kept a book on what you owed. And if you didn't keep one, you'd be cheated and swindled. People started keeping records because they'd say $500 and your book would say $300," and that was pending that you had enough education to maintain a book or the intestinal fortitude to speak out under Jim Crow during the height of the lynching era.

Cousin Truman's account made me realize the many tricks that kept our ancestors economically enslaved regardless of whatever freedom was declared. Would a truly free man need to work himself to death to stay that way?

White widowed women who were left the farms in a will or by inheritance couldn't farm them alone. Brooks Young (of the clan who gave Youngsville, North Carolina its name) made a ½ profit deal with one of my relatives. Truman said you were lucky if you got somebody kind enough to go half. Our relative bought the fertilizer needed to plant and got his half share from the crops, while the widow kept the profits from owning the land.

Truman explained: "There were some good-hearted ones who just gave them land or sold them a lot for a good price. We wouldn't have advanced without a few of those kind around. Some of our family went north, made good money, then came back and found one of the good ones to make a fair deal. One Cousin of mine was sold some nice land by Brooks Young after he helped see about him in his old age, driving him around and tending to his needs; so he sold him a prime piece of land for his service."

But those large landowning Black families became fewer because many got burned out or foreclosed. What was the incentive to stay? When they tried leaving in mass numbers, they were chased down and arrested as an excuse to keep them from taking all that good workforce up north. While being excellent labor, they were not long permitted to hold prominent businesses or seats of office with their skills.

Wilmington, North Carolina, the sight of the first and only coup d'état in US history, set a barrier and provided a blueprint for the whole region long before the more infamous yet similar burn and pillage of Tulsa's

Black Wall Street in Oklahoma. In Wilmington, police, white supremacists, and soldiers brutally massacred at least 60 Black men in 1898. The goal was to end the multi-racial government formed after the Civil War, making the city the most progressive Black majority in the South.

Decades later, when my family and countless other families like ours migrated from the South, the effects of white oppression were all around them, setting limits and conspiring against the possibilities of who the newly freed, formerly enslaved people could be. Those who could hop a train to get out, in some instances, found themselves trapped by debts and prevented from leaving town without paying.

For many Black men like my great-grandfather, the only hope for them and their families was to go north. Even when some returned with enough money to buy, they found few whites willing to sell land to them; others never returned and settled for life anywhere but the segregated South.

Regardless of education level, young Blacks in the South were keenly aware of the advancing and industrially prolific manufacturing age in which they lived. Many had opted out of sitting broke and being disrespected while being exploited by a racist and unjust farming racket, sharecropping, that allowed white families to live comfortably and accrue wealth. In 1953, my great-Uncle, Otis Bumpers, my grandmother's youngest brother, moved from North Carolina to Buffalo, New York, at age 25. These were young men and women with vision and aspirations. And this is not meant to suggest that those who stayed behind were less ambitious. I learned from analyzing my family that both branches, those who migrated north and those who remained in the South, were vital and supported each other. Both were mutually essential for our present-day survival.

Beginning with Sonny-Man in 1940, more of our family migrated north over the next twenty-five years until there was a large city collective, from Washington, DC, to Northern New Jersey, the Oranges, and Newark, New York City, Buffalo, and of course Connecticut. But the one big move that was the most legendary and central to this story occurred in the late 1950s and the early 1960s. My oldest aunts and uncles, some of whom had dropped out of high school, like my Aunt Maxine (Max), who was a teenager then, and my oldest Uncle Jonny Oliver (JO) and oldest Aunt Claudine (Dine), also in their late teens to early 20s; moved up north for a better life. Aunt Dine and Uncle JO had started families already, but Aunt Max went up after them and met her future husband.

From Southern Dirt Roads to Northern Dirty Water

My Aunt Maxine, born in 1944, told me that at 17, she opted out of her last years of segregated schooling in Jim Crow North Carolina to relocate to Waterbury, Connecticut to find work. After a couple of years in Waterbury, she married my Uncle Bruce, from Little Washington, North Carolina, on the coast. She and her husband eventually became entrepreneurs in Waterbury. They owned stores and homes and became landlords aside from working in the factories. In 1963, my Aunt Max's husband, Bruce, and my mother's brother, Uncle Sherrell, drove from Waterbury to Youngsville, North Carolina, to get my grandmother and her seven young daughters.

I wanted to know how ten humans in total and all of their belongings made it out of North Carolina in one car. Uncle Bruce explained that they were all relatively malnourished and "skinny." My grandma and her seven daughters did not have much more than the clothes on their backs, so they all fit easily into his full-sized 1956 Buick Roadmaster. My youngest aunt, Naomi, was just a few months old, and the other girls were pre and early teens. Uncle Bruce and my Uncle Sherrell, 16 years old at the time (who later died in a horrific car accident on January 24, 1997, at the age of 50—another young departure), packed all their belongings in the trunk and on top of the car and drove to Connecticut without looking back. My mom recalled how enamored she was with all the lights and tall buildings while driving through New York City to Connecticut, contrasted with growing up on pitch-black Tarboro Road in Youngsville.

Once they got to Waterbury, they stayed with my Aunt Dine, the mother of my Cousin Tra Mack who was not born yet. My Aunt Dine had three young children between three and a few months old. Aunt Dine's household of five just added my grandmother and her seven daughters to their tiny two-bedroom apartment on Cherry Street, near downtown Waterbury. Most of the houses in this area are gone, but back then, that area was alive and bustling with factories, factory housing, and various other local businesses.

My mother, who was just nine years old when she first arrived in Waterbury, described her first impressions and memories: "I remember getting to Waterbury, and that night, I couldn't sleep because there was so much noise, so much traffic, and so many lights. I wasn't used to that. I remember staying up all night looking out the window just fascinated at everything that was going on in the city," she recalled.

Eventually, my grandmother moved into an apartment with her younger daughters. My grandparents had officially separated, and my grandfather remained in Brooklyn and started another family, adding two more kids to the family tree, my Uncle Michael and my Aunt Jackie. My grandfather often returned to Waterbury for holidays or birthdays, and my grandmother was beyond cordial. The more complicated dynamics of their adult situation and separation didn't register as a kid, especially given the graciousness of my grandmother.

Furthermore, when Grandaddy came from Brooklyn to CT, the family rolled out the red carpet. I did notice that they slept in separate rooms. But given how kind and respectful they were toward each other, my young brain couldn't make sense of their relationship.

There was always a feast, love, laughter, and stories of a past that they had left behind. I can only imagine what he was experiencing seeing all of his grandchildren, who were all in awe and filled with admiration toward him. Grandaddy was a tall, dark, slim man who often donned a gangster brim hat cocked to the side and almost always wore a suit and tie. I never saw my grandad except that he was well-dressed. Truman told me that even during his work on the farm sharecropping, he remembered how sharp he

32

dressed. He left his work as a sharecropper in rural North Carolina for the bright lights of New York on Fifth Avenue and 35th Street. Grandaddy worked at Bond Fifth Avenue, a suit and clothing store in Manhattan, where he helped to dress the stars and the gangsters in and around the city; and, as such, he looked the part. Grandaddy lived on 1895 Bergen Street between Howard Avenue and Saratoga Avenue in Brownsville, Brooklyn, where as a kid, we often visited for holidays or other occasions.

Grandaddy died in 1987 after an extended stay in St. Mary's Hospital in Brooklyn. Our family had his body flown home to North Carolina, which was traditional. I remember our family making the trip south for the funeral when I was 14. Our family bond superseded geographic location, scattered between North and South, New York, New Jersey, Connecticut, and North Carolina. That bond and sense of family was and is the most admirable quality of my family. And although we were a family that did not come from much material wealth, our bond had no monetary value or equivalent, but as a child, it made me feel wealthy, proud, and confident.

My own traumatic life experiences as an adult led me to reflect on my grandfather's experiences, his generation of Black men, and the generations of Black men before them, like Sonny-Man. I tried to imagine the trauma they endured growing up in the Jim Crow South. I simply cannot fathom how they managed and made sense of their trauma. What is even more difficult to fathom is, despite the restrictions imposed under Jim Crow, the degree of grace and love that my grandfather was able to exude in the later years of his life. As a child, I did not understand the life that my elders, like my grandfather, had inherited. All I understood was that they poured love and valuable life lessons into us, despite the common structural, systemic, and repressive obstacles that were a normal part of their entire lives. And little did I know, a version of these same obstacles would emerge for us, living the hopes and dreams of our ancestors up north. Our ancestors' optimism in migrating, and hoping for better for their future generations, extends from a long tradition of *faith*—a hope/vision that life for us will be better than theirs—a legacy they inherited. Their optimism seemed warranted. After all, we were what they had hoped for, the first post-Jim Crow and post-1964 Civil Rights Movement generation of Blacks, the first of our lineage born with all of the rights of US citizens. Nonetheless, we were about to experience what Michelle Alexander termed the New Jim Crow.

But firstly, had my grandad's life gotten better up north because he could wear tailored suits and hats and navigate love and respect between two families? What about my great-grandfather, Sonny-Man, who had moved to New York before him? Having endured a predatory loan scheme that confiscated his father's land, to later escape the toil of sharecropping and discrimination, was the North the paradise they had sought?

Their migration didn't eliminate the structures and practices of oppression and racism—not at all. The police state in the North was just another version of the systematic oppression waiting anywhere Black skin showed up in America.

A Bronx Tale of Police Repression

In the Bronx, where my great-grandfather—Sonny-Man—contributed new branches of our family tree, we witnessed the evidence of racialized, police-state brutality. Dream chasing Blacks fleeing Jim Crow quickly learned that police rhetoric to *protect and serve* did not apply to them. Instead, those who took an oath to protect and serve dehumanized and brutalized Black men, women, and children and terrorized their communities.

A sad example was Eleanor Bumpurs, who gave birth to a daughter by Sonny-Man, and there is some speculation as to whether they were ever officially married. However, she took the other well-known, different spellings of the family name, Bumpers.[1] Eleanor Bumpurs, at the age of 66, made the news in 1984 for her tragic killing at the hands of the New York City Police Department. The Eleanor Bumpurs case pushed the city of NY to the brink of riots.

The case stems from her refusal to pay monthly rent due to repairs needed in her apartment in the Bronx's Sedgwick Houses. Bumpurs, who at the time was elderly, disabled, and deemed "psychotic" due to a social

---

[1] Cousin Truman explained the various spellings of the Bumpers surname. How folks down south spelled based on what they heard phonetically sometimes. Also noted is the fact that Eleanor Bumpurs, although she took his name, was not documented as legally married to Sonny-Man, because he never officially divorced my great grandmother, Lillie Bell Debnam Bumpers.

services visit and psychiatric evaluation at her home, where she was said to be holding a butcher knife defensively ("like a security blanket").

She posed no danger to herself or others. Yet NYPD's six heavily armed policemen must have anticipated an army of violent resistance from the beloved mother and grandmother to her family. Instead of protecting and serving, they came murdering. Eleanor Bumpurs became a tragic symbol of the precariousness of Black life and the hypocrisy of the free and welcoming north.

As a young boy growing up in Connecticut, the Eleanor Bumpurs case, like all NYC news stories, reached us. Southern Connecticut was within the frequency of the local NYC news and radio stations. Many hip-hop artists lamented Eleanor Bumpurs' murder by police, famous actors attended her funeral, and Spike Lee dedicated his film *Do the Right Thing* to her memory. However, I had no other connection to this story until many years later as an adult. As a graduate student, I dedicated my dissertation to my grandmother Dazell Omega Bumpers-Wright, which led to my being contacted by a Michigan State University history professor researching the Bumpurs case. Dr. LaShawn Harris, who incidentally grew up in Sedgwick Houses in the Bronx, uncovered my grandmother's name in the archives as descendants or relatives of Eleanor Williams-Bumpers. Bumpers was also a migrant from Franklin County, North Carolina, who likely knew Sonny-Man and accompanied him to NYC.

Even more intriguing or perhaps scandalous, she was a possible relative, as Debnam's and Williams' (her maiden name) are relatives in Franklin County. Dr. LaShawn Harris, a historian, was researching for a

36

book that historicized police murdering Black women, spearheaded by the Bumpurs case. A Google search led her to my dissertation, which I had dedicated to my grandmother. Dr. Harris was able to contact me through mutual acquaintances we shared from my time as a graduate student at Michigan State University.

My grandma had passed two years prior, but my mother and her siblings were unaware that their grandfather, Sonny-Man, had a family line in New York all those years. I immediately shared what I had learned with my mom. Meanwhile, the daughter of Ms. Eleanor Bumpurs was unaware of her father's large family in Connecticut. This story added another layer to my family saga fleeing Jim Crow, only to find equally harsh realities up north.

The turmoil of my family—what they had to endure as sharecroppers, and the land they had that banks and wealthy whites took from them through an array of predatory loan schemes and other "legal" harassments—is a much more common American tragedy than is documented or analyzed. The decades of toiling with absolutely nothing to show for it except literally the clothes on their backs when they migrated was something I learned as an adult through my research. The years that my family faced these traumatic horrors were never mentioned to me while growing up. They never complained of any of these old troubles, and it never occurred to me as a child what their life was like living in the Jim Crow South. They all longed to return, and many of them did.

Raised by an Honorable and Resilient Clan

Suppose I had to describe my family who migrated, consisting of my grandmother, aunts, uncles, and all who came before us. Words like "regal" and "integrity" come to mind. Considering all they had endured living under Jim Crow, they never spoke badly about white people as reasonably could be imagined. They weren't naïve to the systemic, recurring racism; they were visionaries and people of deep faith who instilled the same in us. You heard only snippets of what they endured, but mostly they just worked and provided for their family and looked forward, choosing to try and forget or erase the traumatic episodes of violence and dehumanization.

They didn't foresee going from slave patrols and caravans of lynch mobs in the South to the local police patrols acting as an occupying force all around us in the North. They couldn't say, "This is how you handle white authority up north . . . " because it was all new to them. They couldn't envision the life we inherited up north. My generation experienced new and updated versions of what our elders fled from in the South, *modern* versions of Jim Crow.

Our elders found themselves watching my generation deal with new struggles in our own way. They witnessed all that brought them there and into the middle-class become worthless to their offspring, us. For example, offshoring the factories prevented my generation from inheriting any of our ancestors' contributions to the industrial boom. By the time my generation came of age, the manufacturing industry was a shell of itself. And filling the vacuum was street life and an underground economy that included drugs and the drug trade of the 1980s and 1990s. And crack soon became king.

Our fore folks could not have anticipated what their future generations would inherit and didn't know how to direct us. My elder aunts told me that during the sharecropping peak season, they weren't allowed to go to school; instead, they toiled on the farm from their earliest memories to their teen and adult years. All they knew was work. When I asked her about school, my mother's oldest sister, my Aunt Dine, Tra's mom, recalled: "If the white man said we couldn't go to school, we didn't go. All we did was work."

That hard work ethic is all they had, which they took up north into the manufacturing jobs they found. That hard work ethic they applied to the new lives they learned to live and how they raised their children. It worked for them and translated nicely into the ongoing US economic and industrial revolution, it upgraded their class to a level they had dreamed of and imagined while living in the South. Due to their circumstances, they offered only marginal insight regarding economic and sociopolitical advancement. My generation weren't farmers, we weren't from the South, and we hadn't worked in factories, and our elders didn't have a template beyond that. Whatever they had left when they died and any lessons they could leave behind for us was all we got—Southern values, integrity, family, and love.

The children of the Great Migration, my family at least, inherited little to no economic wealth, not much education, and little guidance towards any. We did not inherit much wisdom or advice on navigating bigoted police patrols. My cousins and I agreed that what that generation gave us was obvious. They made sure we understood how to fight— physically, mentally, emotionally, and spiritually. And violations of our bodies and physical space were resisted and often met with major confrontations. We could not come running to our grandmother's house because somebody had chased us from school. Our elders commanded that we defend ourselves. Our whole clan understood the art of fighting back, something their generations living in the Jim Crow South, forbidden by law, could scarcely do.

As an adult, I learned that America has always been a battleground where the fight for Black liberty and life could lead to death. For Blacks in the US to flourish without the omnipresent patronization of white interference is perceived as a national security threat. For example, the powerful resistance to the Civil Rights Movement of the 1960s is reflected in today's rollback of many of those civil rights gains and others under threat of repeal. The Immigration Act of 1964, affirmative action, and voting rights were all monumental civil rights acts.

The other thing our elders passed down was their specific Southern values. All of my cousins and I had certain things instilled in us from birth, like respect. You'd get fucked up talking back to an aunt, even by one of the cousins, no matter how gangster or tough you were. We were raised to respect our elders, especially family members. Also, outsiders or non-family members who violated or disrespected any of our family were addressed. I interpret these as amended Southern values instilled in us by my grandma that centered around respect.

For example, I had a high school guidance counselor who told me that by the time I was 21, I "would have a criminal record as long as my arm or be dead." At age 17, I was furious for her to say that to me. I thought in my mind, "Fuck you, bitch!" but it would have been out of character to say that, even if that's what I felt in my 17-year-old soul. Yes, the fight was there, but so were specific values. Those family values were channel into adulthood because it was a new kind of fight happening up north. We wound up in a police state, and our neighborhoods and communities were under constant occupation. Our ancestors had no language for that and no strategies for the economic traps, deindustrialization accompanied by tidal waves of cocaine, a burgeoning crack epidemic, and mass incarceration. They couldn't help us through this new version of oppression with anything but what they gave us.

These are stories of my family's migration. They left everything behind for the possibility of a better life for themselves and their future generations. Reflecting upon these stories led me from the roots up to myself and my cousins' generation. After 1964, with rights our elders had never known, and Jim Crow but an old whisper—we emerged. But what would these new sons of Waterbury, navigating Dirty Water, be like with so much freedom and in the shadows of dying factories as their only inheritance?

CHAPTER THREE
Our Inheritance

It occurred to me that no matter where I lived, geography could
not save me . . .
– Wilkerson

We inherited Waterbury. A place passed on to us by ancestors seeking
refuge from a murderous and oppressive Jim Crow South. Nonetheless, my
earliest recollections of Waterbury are memorable. Beautiful natural
landscape, hills and greenery, and the most amazing fall foliage. As a child,
growing up in the North End was joyful and magical in many ways,
particularly in the years before the crack era. Crisscrossing the city,
discovering parks and neighborhoods other than ours was a big part of my
childhood. In the North End, pear, apple, crabapple trees, and grapevines
were prevalent. Neighbors were neighborly, and the community looked
after the kids, and everyone knew everyone and each other's families. Many
of our grandparents, aunts, and uncles knew one another from back in the
South. Then came crack, and it seemed as though the most joyous
memories died along with all the pretty trees and their fruits.

I loved growing up in Waterbury—it was a great experience, and it
gave me the foundation for the man who I eventually became. In hindsight,
thirty-something years later, as an academic with a reflective memory and

other critical tools and insights, I am able to recollect the past and deconstruct the changes that transformed the city.

From birth until I graduated high school I lived in the livest, Blackest corners of the city: The Bowl, Bishop and Walnut Streets. Historically, these blocks provided refuge for Blacks migrating to Waterbury. I was born in the building located at 1853 North Main Street on top of the Sugar Bowl restaurant. Long after the restaurant closed the area became known as the Sugar Bowl, and eventually "The Bowl." Located at the intersection of North Main and East Farm Streets. The Bowl was the central point of the city's Black culture. Willow and Bishop Streets are to the west of The Bowl; Walnut Street and Long Hill Projects to the east; Lakewood was north; and the North Square was south of The Bowl. If you placed these neighborhoods on a map, which are main arteries of the city's Black life line, The Bowl is smack in the middle. The Bowl attracted the most colorful and vibrant characters in the city and offered every kind of activity and entertainment common in urban Black culture. I left The Bowl at around age 8 for an equally live section several blocks to the northwest, on Bishop Street across from Fulton Park, and then eventually back to the northeast part of the city, on Rose Street off of Walnut Street at around age 17.

School Daze

My introduction to K-12 was Slocum Elementary School, the neighborhood school which incorporated many of the neighborhoods from around The Bowl. Halfway through my kindergarten year, my mother decided to relocate to North Carolina. Although I was young, the move seemed abrupt, and I remember feeling confused at the thought of leaving all of my cousins. I later understood that my mom was concerned about my biological father's deep involvement with New York City street life. She became aware that people were after him or wanted to kill him. Perhaps overreacting, she felt concerned, even though they were not a couple. The mother of my biological father, Stanley "Butch" Minor, had moved from NYC to Connecticut for a job in the 1970s, but my father never joined her. He visited periodically from New York, which was how he had met my mother.

I have sporadic memories of my father. I vaguely remember riding the subway in NYC as a child and going ice skating at Rockefeller Plaza. But those who knew him most described him as a fly, well-dressed, pretty boy from Harlem with a boxing pedigree. He was not very tall but thorough enough to navigate the NYC streets and he managed to woo my mom, a stunningly beautiful and elegant 17–18-year-old when they met. He was a couple of years older than her, and only after I was born did my mom realize the extent of his involvement with the streets of NYC, and she wanted no parts of it.

Nonetheless, we were on a Greyhound bus headed to North Carolina in the middle of my kindergarten year, and I didn't understand why. As a child, I hated rural North Carolina, partly because vast chunks of my summer were spent there. Plus, I hated the long ten-plus-hour drive and the time away from my friends during summers in Waterbury. I recall the eerie feeling I got looking at the old plantations and derelict farmhouses, shacks, barns, and all of the places where enslavement and sharecropping thrived. In the 1970s and 1980s, these traumatic relics still stood, and although, as a child, I didn't have the knowledge or language, but these historical monuments made me uncomfortable. Perhaps I was genetically triggered by my ancestors' traumatic experiences?

I spent the last half of my kindergarten year enrolled in Youngsville Elementary School in Youngsville, North Carolina. My memory is vague, except I recall there were many white people, the school seemed huge, and I felt lost. I also recall being happy when the summer came, and my mother said we were going back to Waterbury.

When I returned to Waterbury, I re-enrolled in Slocum where I stayed for the first grade and second grade, which was the last year before it closed down. The mostly Black students from Slocum were divided up and sent to three different schools. I was part of a busload of students that went to Regan Elementary, where I began third grade. I had not known any of the Regan kids except my neighborhood friends and neighbors who went to Slocum. Regan was much more integrated than Slocum; I remember there were lots more white kids at Regan, but still a fair amount of Black students. The Black and Puerto Rican students at Regan were kids from Lakewood Projects. Lakewood was also on North Main Street about ten blocks north of the Bowl. Kids were territorial at that time and the Sugar Bowl kids carried a reputation which made for a lot of tension.

I can't say that I befriended many of the kids at Regan. One day during class, I got into a fight with one kid named Johnny Noble (J. Noble). J. Noble was a young general and was clearly calling the shots amongst his third-grade peers before I got there. He approached me aggressively, and I did not back down and we ended up exchanging eight-year-old blows. Our third-grade teacher took us to the principal's office. I recall the school principal, a goofy white man with glasses who, upon hearing that we had gotten into a fight, thought himself humorous and shouted, "You're out! Three days!" like he was an umpire in a *friendly game of baseball*. No probing questions nor discussions toward reconciliation between us, and no leadership. "You're out!" was his solution—a three-day suspension. This was my first experience with what I would later describe as a school culture lacking care and compassion, a fundamentally missing component in the school experience of young Black boys in schools, then and now. The principal did not understand that his lack of understanding of the pervasive Black and Puerto Rican culture in his school, which I am certain he had no respect for, could have led to much bigger problems for him. His oversight, disinterest, or perhaps his arrogance could have led to stoking the flames that could easily set his school on fire or spilled off into our communities between two rival neighborhoods. Fortunately, that did not happen, but the principal's actions or inactions created a pathway of which he was completely oblivious. A few years later, by the time we reached high school, J. Noble had been arrested and convicted for multiple murders.

Needless to say I had to face my mother when I got home regarding my suspension. I was terrified. I remember thinking, "I might die today; she's gonna kill me." When I got home, she asked, "What happened?" (even though she had already received the call from school), I told her, I stood up to a bully and she just looked at me and said, "That's alright because you're going to Sacred Heart next year."

I remember thinking, "Damn." I would've preferred the belt instead of transferring to a Catholic school with a uniform requirement. We were not Catholic, but on the East Coast Catholic schools, in most cases, were the only private school alternatives and non-Catholics paid higher tuition. The following year, I started fourth grade at Sacred Heart Grammar School (SHGS) wearing my green slacks and my yellow button-up shirt with my green plaid tie.

The Sacred Heart in the Hood

Sacred Heart would introduce me to one of my best and life-long friends, William Wilson. We called him Will. Will's parents had migrated from Jamaica, and like me, he was born in Waterbury in the North End, near The Bowl. Prior to meeting him at Sacred Heart, I remembered him and his brother were the neighborhood newspaper delivery boys. It'd be freezing, and he and his brother would be out delivering newspapers, rain, sleet, or snow. Will's parents were strict and in our young age I only remembered seeing him outside either delivering papers or going to or leaving church. But when I got to Sacred Heart, we became instant friends.

Our friendship started after a fistfight over a coat hanger outside of the classroom. Once again, fighting meant exchanging fourth-grade blows and kicks and neither of us backed down. *Ok, good, so he ain't no punk, and he's going to fight, and he's from the neighborhood . . .* , I thought at the time. From that moment in fourth grade through our eighth-grade year, he became my best friend.

My Aunt Maxine had three kids—two girls, Cynthia and Nina, and one boy, Derreck (D-Pruden). Recall, Aunt Maxine is my mom's big sister, who at 17 years old took the initiative that brought my grandmother and her seven youngest daughters out of Youngsville in 1963. Aunt Max was a hustler and the most entrepreneurial in my family. She and her husband had multiple jobs and businesses. They owned the three-family house that they lived in, other rental properties, and a small grocery store. Even still, they worked multiple jobs, my aunt was a part-time school bus driver in the mornings, and worked in the factory in the evening, and my Uncle Bruce was a DJ who also worked in the factory. They had a great work ethic and they put my Cousin Derreck, who was three years older than me, into Sacred Heart all of his K–12 years. He was the only one in my family out of my boy cousins, at that point, to attend private school his whole school-age years.

I took solace going to school with my Cousin D-Pruden, who was closest to me in age. Neither of us had brothers (although he had two older sisters), so he became my big brother. When I arrived at Sacred Heart and started fourth grade, he was starting seventh grade.

Sacred Heart introduced me to another side of Waterbury. I met kids from different environments, white kids from big houses with huge yards and basketball courts in their driveways. That was less common for

Black kids back then. This was also my first experience with integration. I think I can look back and say that a sensible amount of mutual respect and friendship was established. What I can say now in reflection is that seeing white kids with more resources and bigger houses back then was not a source of envy, and I never felt like what I had wasn't enough. I never felt I lived in the wrong communities, and I never felt like my family wasn't good enough. I never wanted to be white or wished I was; I always felt comfortable with myself. I can't say that I had the language back then, but in hindsight, I can say that I was proud to be Black and I valued the love from my family and our community.

Besides, I lived in the livest and most vibrant communities where the energy was palpable, the music was good, the people were witty, funny and intelligent. But Sacred Heart widened my life lens, especially as I came to understand racial differences. I didn't interact much or befriend white kids in my previous public schools. Mainly, it seemed as though kids just gravitated to what was familiar. But at Sacred Heart, not all but a select few white kids became my friends. Some of us interacted outside of school, and I got to know some of their parents, and when reflecting on racism in those times, nothing immediately jumped out at me. I could've misunderstood or overlooked some things as my mind was too young to understand or articulate the nuances of racism, but there wasn't anything blatant. I was never called a nigger by a friend or acquaintance. I didn't feel energy like that like from kids with whom I established mutual respect.

The Death of a Father

In September 1982, just as I was beginning fourth grade at Sacred Heart, my mom pulled me into the back room of my grandmother's place on Orange Street and closed the door. She pulled out a newspaper article that read, "New York City Man Shot and Killed." She read the article, the details of which I do not remember, but the crux was that my biological father was shot and killed in Harlem. My mom's premonition that drove us to North Carolina four years earlier had come to pass. I had an estranged relationship with my biological father, a mysterious figure whose mention was taboo.

In May 1986, toward the end of seventh grade, my tall, dark, and fly grandfather George Oliver Wright, aka Plook, died. Grandaddy had sought refuge from Jim Crow, faithful in a better future for himself and all of his offspring, like so many of his peers and those before them. Willing to risk everything to keep their children from second-class citizenship, they settled in the very cold, fast-paced, urban Northeast. Much different from the humidity in rural North Carolina. Did my grandparents run from, in essence, a different version of the very same oppressive violence that would plague their future progeny (my generation)? Grandaddy's death coincided with a significant life shift for me, our family, and the entire region in the Northeast where my family sought refuge. Unforeseeable danger and trouble was brewing. Our new lives up north were getting closer to an uncertain and tumultuous future reflective of the past.

Those puzzles, losses, and left turns were softened by memories of my mom singing in church, around the house, in the car, and anywhere there was an audience. Luther Vandross was her favorite and he quickly became one of my favorites, too. My mom's boyfriend when I was born was James White; we called him White. White was, tall, dark, handsome, and always well-dressed. Although he was not my biological father and not the man who my mother married, he was a great dude, and treated me like his own son, and I loved him for that. At the beginning of the school year, even after he and my mother were no longer together, he would search me out to buy me school clothes. He did this annually until the year I graduated from high school. He did this even though he and my mom had not been a couple since I was in kindergarten.

I am pointing out the various ways that strong Black men showed up in my life, just as many others were dying off. I always felt a sense of stability despite the various moves, and the life-altering lessons on the horizon.

****

High School at a Crossroad

I wanted to attend the local public schools bad. And I plotted ways to get kicked out of Sacred Heart, but I would never cross that line because my mother would've killed me. And I wouldn't be here to tell these stories.

I always wanted to be with my people from the North End and attend the schools that served the kids from the Sugar Bowl, Lakewood, and the city's other live areas. Sacred Heart just did not suit my personality. Upon eighth-grade graduation from Sacred Heart Grammar School

51

(SHGS), my life came to another crossroad—I had to choose high schools. It was either the local hood favorite, Wilby High School, or Sacred Heart High School (SHHS). And my Mom was forcing my hand toward Sacred Heart High.

A pre-entry exam was required to enroll in SHHS. And most of my friends from SHGS were attending Sacred Heart High School like my friend Will, but a few others were entering public schools.

About that Sacred Heart entry exam. Information was mailed home with dates and instructions. But that mail and its information never made it to my mother. I checked the mail every day that summer and when the entry exam information came, I never gave it to her. The deadline came and went and I never took the test. My mom was so busy with work and life that when she remembered to inquire, "What's going on with the test for Sacred Heart?" I informed her, "Oh, we missed the deadline."

"What do you mean?" she asked me, and I replied, "I don't know, I just know we missed it. I'm going to have to go to one of those public schools, I guess." Mom agreed to allow me to go to Wilby for one year but threatened that if I got into trouble or if my grades slipped she'd be pulling me out. I knew that I only had to survive for one year, and then I'd be in the clear because SHHS didn't accept transfers after sophomore year, which is ironic because it was after my freshman year when life took some hard turns.

Wilby was everything I imagined. The whole state and many across the nation were buzzing due to Wilby basketball my first year. By 1988, Waterbury was also becoming engulfed by crack smoke. Cocaine and the crack epidemic reshaped much of our childhood focus on city parks and pear trees toward opportunities to cash in on a market driven by addiction and the destruction of our communities and neighborhoods. Crack showed up in our neighborhoods unannounced, and many of the city's Black innovators and entrepreneurs unwittingly transitioned into this drug trade. The crack epidemic sucked in many of our most entrepreneurial and savviest, sharp-minded hustlers and many of our most charismatic personalities. As the factories closed, a new economy emerged.

CHAPTER FOUR

Generation X: The First Black Americans Constitutionally Recognized as Full Citizens—AKA the Superpredators

> Our Negro problem, therefore, is not of the Negro's making . . .
> – Wilkerson

I was enamored by the streets and street life growing up. My earliest memories of being *outside* and running around were with my older cousins. We would meet up at a central location, usually my grandmother's house, and walk across town from the North End to the East End of town to the Boys Club. We would pass through neighborhoods and encounter kids who were unfamiliar to us. Growing up, the Boys Club was the meeting point for the city's most talented athletes and where unfamiliar kids from different neighborhoods gathered and became friends. The Waterbury Boys Club was where your mettle was tested and where reputations emerged—from fighting, playing basketball, being cool, or funny.

I started going to the Boys Club around age six or seven. Boys Club reputations carried us throughout our adolescent years, into high school and beyond. Before crack, I was shaped by Boys Club activities, local parks playing basketball, hanging out in front of The Bowl watching traffic, or from walking the neighborhoods with friends. The four seasons in New England offered different activities. The winter meant epic snowball fights and bumper-car sledding. Summer time was summer league basketball, and pick-up games in the parks. During fall it was tackle football in the parks. Street life and culture was very different before crack. But crack hit the scene and caused a paradigm-shift of seismic proportions.

For whatever reasons, Wilby High School seemed like the school where most of my peers interested in this new crack hustle ended up. The liveliest kids from the most vibrant neighborhoods went to Wilby. Wilby had the best conversationalists, storytellers, and basketball players, and the prettiest Black and Puerto Rican girls in the city. For my peers and me, these experiences were about a quest and a zest for life.

To be noticed or popular at Wilby, you had to be built a certain way; meaning you were unique and had confidence. Many kids avoided the school because there was too much going on. I ran to it! I was born, raised, and nurtured around the Sugar Bowl. The word "Live" was the only theme playing out around me. It was like I genetically craved all of that colorful life with all of the ambiance and everything that came with it. But as a young teenager, I was not looking with an eye to the future, at the politics of those failing schools and curriculums with educators who didn't care about us. Many whom didn't have our best interest at heart, didn't really understand us, and in some respects didn't even like us. As a kid in the middle of it, I couldn't see the bigger picture. I knew which teachers I couldn't trust (most of them), those who didn't care (nearly all of them), and those to avoid, and I respected the ones who took a genuine interest in me and where I came from. These were the exceptions.

In Black and hip-hop culture, the connotation of "street-life" or being "in the streets" requires an identification of certain traits and qualities. For example, navigating and overcoming some type of hardship. Resistance against oppressive circumstances, systems, and people. Making a way from no way, and bare bones survival. Much of these qualities are inherent and passed on through DNA of Blacks in the US. You can take someone out of the streets, but the survival qualities that were inherited that helped them survive and even thrive in the streets will shine through. You can cover or polish it, but it remains beneath the surface. Street people or street life often conjure negativity, but negativity exists in every environment and every community. However, there are also values, norms, mores, codes, and shared ways of believing and knowing, an aspect of street culture rarely given any credence.

There are hierarchies and various posts in the streets. There are strong men and women who work as regulators or security, intellectuals, economists and financiers, philanthropists, comedians, and peacemakers. Often one individual wears one or several of these hats. In my case, these environmental influences—the good, bad, and ugly—raised a boy into a man. Waterbury's North End streets were nothing but action, as number runners, pimps, prostitutes, and local drug dealers shared the city's sidewalks with local educators, medical, and various other professionals. I witnessed all of this just outside of my door. As a young child, these are just the neighbors. Many of these larger-than-life figures, who seemed unapproachable, I learned were very accessible and cordial. Most of them were highly intelligent, but through various circumstances found themselves, whether by force or preference, living a life underground.

Growing up, I heard many legendary stories about the old school guys, identifiable around town by a variety of luxury cars like Rolls Royce and Mercedes Benz. These individuals made the city live. Pre-crack, these individuals controlled Waterbury streets. As decadent as it might sound to anyone unfamiliar, Waterbury for its inner-city residents was fun and community-oriented. In our segregated neighborhoods of Black, Puerto Rican, Cape Verdean, Jamaican, and others from various Caribbean islands, it was all love for the most part. By and large, we were extended family. We inter-dated, inter-married, had kids together, and this is how it was for a mixed neighborhood of second-generation *refugees*. Yes, the Blackamericans who fled the Jim Crow South were refugees, too!

Waterbury BC and AC: Before Crack and After Crack

Then, out of nowhere, crack cocaine came and changed everything. I have vivid memories of life in Waterbury, BC—Before Crack. Life before everything changed. We witnessed individuals who were pillars in our community become addicted. The strongest men and women in our communities began smoking crack and became a shell of themselves. I've had conversations with rehabilitated crack addicts who recalled that when crack arrived it was presented as not much different than weed; it was just another way to get high. Crack was initially promoted and marketed as a new fad, a trend, and something cool to try. Crack attracted mostly kids and young adults who had no understanding or foresight of how addictive it was.

Cocaine flooded our city like a tsunami; ransacked households, and washed away an entire generation of Black dignity and integrity. Crack smoke became infused with the summer breeze. The smell of crack was easily discernible and it was everywhere. It replaced the smell of crabapples in the summertime of our youth with the rot of potential. And consequently, this single drug devastated our communities and neighborhoods, seemingly irreversibly. As for my involvement, I never used it, smoked it, or snorted anything, but I sold it. In hindsight, I am not proud of my choice to get involved. In the 1990s, crack involvement was popular, ubiquitous, and pervasive in Black communities—you were smoking it if you weren't selling it. On the heels of deindustrialization and factory jobs, which had brought our ancestors to the city, no longer an economic alternative, crack was a viable substitute for those of us who chose that route. And there were many of us. In my opinion, crack set Blackamerican advancement back decades.

The crack epidemic transformed the whole concept of what it meant to hustle in our community's lexicon. The migrants to Waterbury were hard workers with major aspirations. Whether that meant working several jobs and learning trades along the way. Elders in Black communities possessed an array of trades, skills, and premonitions to learn new skills that they passed on to later generations. Every Black community and many Black families knew handymen with every requisite skillset. Auto-mechanics, painters, construction workers, every sort of trade and repair, modeling and remodeling needed was easily accessible. These trades and skills were handed down from generations of Black laborers in the South. But crack destroyed much of the oral traditions and learning by doing prevalent in Black communities, particularly in Waterbury. The desire to learn these trades as careers or side hustles quickly dissipated as the crack market and its economy ballooned. Before crack, hustling resembled what my aunts and other migrant relatives did. They worked in the factory at night, saved money, bought rental properties; took that income and opened neighborhood mom-and-pop stores, employed their kids, nieces and nephews. Or worked in the factory, and on the weekends or in the evening took calls for various handy-work like plumbing and auto mechanics. My uncles and many of the men in my family were auto mechanics and could be found in one of my uncle's neighborhood auto repair shops. After crack, to hustle meant to get that same kind of income—and much more—faster, with less effort, and no skill or trade required.

The night of October 18, 2018 I sat with my Cousin Tra reminiscing. Cancer had reduced him to a shadow of the man who I grew up admiring and mimicking. Tra was the closest person to me who I watched, with my own eyes, transform his life by the drug trade. In his early twenties, Tra was one of the biggest crack hustlers in the city. Like so many others from Generation X on the East Coast, the first generation of Southern Blacks, post-Civil Rights, born up north and with all of the rights granted by the US Constitution. Ironically, this is also the first generation of mass incarceration or the *New Jim Crow*. Tra Mack had unlimited potential and talent—whatever he chose to do, he excelled. Looking back, it's unfortunate that those talents went in that direction. But when juxtaposed with the gaps in school preparation, curriculums, role models, resources, connections to other possibilities, and opportunities withheld or unavailable, what were the other viable options? They didn't exist for the vast majority of us. The rarer exceptions existed, but they were just that— rare.

It wasn't hard for me at 14 years old—grandfather and unknown biological dad both deceased just a few years before, absent paternal guidance and surrounded by the aroma of the streets—to look up to a relative who was not just living, but LIVE! Seeing how popular he was and how the drug game had transformed his life, I aspired to do the same. You didn't need a high school or college degree, a factory 9-to-5, or be put on by inheritance from anybody. Back then, all you needed was some street credibility, some heart, a willingness to take a risk, and hustle—Tra Mack had all of that in spades.

In his early 20s, Tra had a condo, a Benz, a BMW, and a Chevy Blazer truck. Gucci, gold, and all of the latest fashion. He came with all the bells and whistles of the late 1980s, early 1990s hustler. Whatever that looked like, that was him. Many of his peers and some elders were jealous of him and at the same time feared him, but for us, his family, and close circle, he was still just Tra. For the most part, he was the Tra we always knew and had grown up with; he just had way more money, perhaps more than anyone in my family. Tra was not trying to involve me in that game, but I was already plotting my entry.

Yo! How Can I Be Down?

At around age 14, an older dude, a local DJ from the neighborhood around the Bowl approached me. He said, "Yo, since you're out here, why don't you take this package and make some money?" I was immediately down— "Hell yeah, what I gotta do?" I asked, even though I kind of knew what to do because I had been watching it from afar. So when this local DJ from the neighborhood pulled up in his fancy car, I did not hesitate. I weighed the risk and rewards and settled for the opportunity. He offered a 60/40 profit split; better than my ancestors 75/25 sharecropping split and far less work and humiliation. I accepted his offer. And like clockwork, I was on, and in the game. After a few days I had extra spending money, and soon after more money than my young mind could have imagined.

During my freshman year at Wilby High School, my life took a drastic turn. I studied the streets more than any subject in class, and I got pretty good at it. I got to the point where at 14 to 15 years old, I started to understand the economics of the new street hustle. I started looking for ways to cut out the middleman, the neighborhood DJ, and find a strong New York plug. Back then the plugs to the cartels were mostly centralized in NYC.

I cut out the local DJ after a few flips with him and approached my Cousin Tra. Tra was not interested in involving me but it was too late. Tra had realized that without his help I was already on. So with money in hand, I asked him for his New York plug. I already understood all of the measurements and prices. Tra, sensing my understanding and ambition, agreed to help me. "Alright, I'll do it." I handed him $2,500. Perhaps in his mind, he concluded, "Well, if you're gonna do it, let me help you." And before long, I had a small enterprise. I had Tra Mack's plug and some of my older cousins working for me, and some of their friends, too. These were all older guys, like 19 to 21, and they're working for me, a 14–15-year-old still in high school.

After a short while, I showed up to school looking the part—jewelry, money-stacks, fresh sneakers—and I thought I was the shit. That was my narrow mind at the time; developing in the petri dish of the streets, a product of a narrow worldview. But that was my reality.

The Un-Holy Trinity: Deindustrialization, Mass Incarceration, and Political Corruption

I'm not proud of my contribution to destroying our community and neighborhoods. But there's a lot of room for blame. Many people need to take ownership of what happened to Waterbury. And it certainly does not start at the bottom in the city's poorest, most divested, under-resourced communities, schools and neighborhoods. It starts at the very top. You've got political corruption at the highest scale in Waterbury—probably more than anywhere else in the United States. Political scandals and corruption involving government and elected officials in the city in the 1990s and 2000s were commonplace. So what we were doing at a street level mirrored, fractionally, what was happening at the top. Within the space of two decades between the 1990s and 2000s, Waterbury had two mayors who were both separately indicted and convicted for graft and other criminal charges while in office.

The first mayor, Joseph J. Santopietro, was convicted during my senior year of high school. The second mayor, Phillip Giordano, followed a few short years afterward. A few years after these two mayoral scandals, Connecticut's governor, John J. Rowland, also a son of Waterbury, was indicted and convicted while sitting governor. But Waterbury's political corruption predates my family's and many others' migration story. The city's first national scandal occurred at the onset of World War II, with Waterbury's debonaire Mayor T. Frank Hayes, who served between 1930 and 1939. Hayes was ultimately convicted for money laundering and steering city money to shadowy contractors. Several other of the state's major urban cities were similarly held hostage by these kinds of scandals, over the past several decades, to which national publications began referring to Connecticut as *Corrupticut*.

A School-to-Prison Floodgate

For many of us, school was just a pastime. We were all heading to prison inevitably, as most school counselors and educators consistently found ways to remind us. Waterbury public schools were like a placeholder for kids until they were old enough for prison. When we graduated, it seemed as if almost everyone headed for the streets. School did not prepare us for much else. We were going nowhere, and a culture of acceptance of these realities permeated our school system and city politics. Except for the few exceptional athletes who managed to stay in schools, few of us went to college. So many of my talented peers were stopped in their tracks by the allure of the streets, and the doldrum presented to us as education.

Legendary tales of Wilby High School resonated throughout my childhood. My mom went there, as well as several of my aunts and many cousins. Also Wilby boasted some of the city's most legendary basketball teams and players. Waterbury is arguably the basketball capital of the state of Connecticut. I was at Wilby the same time as one of the state's most iconic and legendry players, Phil Lott.

Phil Lott was a senior my freshman year at Wilby. He was a 6'4" or 6'5" point guard with a big frame, physically gifted, a national phenom, and a highly coveted blue-chip recruit. Phil was a man playing with high school boys, who seemed to get better every year, and each year he added an element to his game as a testament to his work ethic. While in high school, he played and excelled against the Division I college players and the pros in the local summer league.

As one of the leading scorers in the nation, Phil was part of a talented crop of players from Connecticut getting national attention. Connecticut players were fertile ground for UCONN under Jim Calhoun but even more so for UMass under Coach John Calipari, where he got his first big start. Calipari brought in several marquee guys from the state. Phil was ahead of his time and a rare breed, and neither UMass nor UCONN at that time had a player of Phil's stature. I recall my freshman year something

64

that is common now but unheard of back then—all of Connecticut's media, TV and newspapers, converged on Wilby's campus to hear Phil announce where he would play college basketball. Phil stood at a podium set up for him in the school library with cameras flashing, donning the now classic Louis Vuitton, LV, jacket. Phil departed from most everyone's expectations and announced that he'd be attending the University of Hawaii after many in the state speculated he'd attend UCONN. Phil had a stellar career at Hawaii, where he scored over 1,000 points for his college career, but fought through some nagging injuries.

I myself had a relatively productive high school basketball career at Wilby as well. Phil had given the legendary Coach Reggie O'Brien his first league and city championship. And four years later during my senior year, we gave him his second. My years playing ball at Wilby were interrupted because I stood on the corners in my neighborhood hustling and selling drugs instead of going to school. I was young and charismatic, fearless with a drive and respect from my peers and older dudes. Channeled better, maybe I could have gone further as an athlete. Phil had set the bar high and I had little interest in playing basketball as a career.

But I got what I wanted. I attended the 'hood-famous Wilby High School. I made a name for myself while I was there and long after I graduated. In hindsight, however, the lack of quality curriculum and educators who understood us, our communities, and culture contributed to some of the brightest minds at Wilby distrusting and disengaging from school, including me. This school culture of low expectations permeating urban cities and schools throughout the US, to me, is an American tragedy. The drug trade at this time seemed like a sensible alternative, as the scope of the destructive force of selling and using drugs was not quite in full-focus. Or at least the benefit/rewards of destroying Black communities and young lives like mine was overwhelmingly an attractive risk to take.

Deindustrialization superseded local politics. It was a geopolitical arrangement between corporations and national level politics at a huge national expense. Like so many manufacturing centered cities, Waterbury never recovered from deindustrialization and as a result, lost so much potential. So many bright minds and brilliant people failed to develop and evolve in part due to a broken and failed school system, unprecedented political scandal, and corruption, along with an intentional divestment from the communities where we lived. Luckily for me, something happened that derailed my tenure selling drugs—I got arrested as a 16-year-old juvenile, a minor, and my first offense. I was a relatively good high school basketball player, and I played for a coach who cared about kids like me. The inner-city kids who were bright with determination, heart, and respect, Coach Reggie O'Brien looked out for us.

I ended up in Waterbury Superior Court with letters of support written on my behalf. Coaches, teachers, community members that my mom had connections to all conveyed the message: *He's a good kid, he made a mistake, and deserves another chance.* The judge was clear. *Once school ends, I will send you to Manson Youth Institute (MYI) in Cheshire, Connecticut* (a jail for boys and young men between 14 and 21) during the summer months. The summer I spent at MYI opened my eyes. I recall seeing only one white kid at MYI; everyone else was Black and Puerto Rican. Although I could hold my own and carry my own weight, it was a welcomed sight to see guys who I knew from Waterbury, neighbors, and family-friends who had rank and pull in MYI. MYI inspired a new train of thought in me, basically: *Fuck this shit. I don't want this life.* Luckily, I had basketball to fall back on and a coach who believed in me. But who was I kidding, the streets were in my DNA. I was a street dude through and through.

Hip Hop: Heirs of a Black Radical Tradition

Growing up, the streets and hip-hop music were synonymous. Street codes and hip-hop music co-created norms that represented much of the complexities of Blackness and the Black urban experience of my generation in the US. In my view, the first generation after the Civil Rights Movement were primed and ready to advance the causes of their heroes. Generation X were the heirs of the Black radical elements within the Civil Rights Movement. We were inspired by and cut from similar cloth as Malcolm X, the Black Panther Party, even Martin Luther King Jr., and other Black revolutionaries across the Americas, Africa, and the Caribbean. But we were easily identified, targeted, and quickly disenfranchised in the US. Nonetheless, a large number from the first generation after the Civil Rights Movement, particularly those of us whose ancestors migrated from the South, were informed by the streets.

These experiences and world views, along with ambition, cultivated a creative genius from which emerged a powerful political platform: hip hop culture. This new political platform represented alternative world views and possibilities, which we could express and exercise without any Eurocentric input, interference, or approval. Hip-hop music was the voice and consciousness of the streets. The streets—Black urban culture— despised by white mainstream America and ignored by bourgeois Blacks, suddenly had a national platform, which quickly became global. Unfortunately, this global, multi-billion dollar cash cow was subsequently commandeered by vulture-like corporations and their minions. The organic pathways and trajectories being crafted by hip hop were manipulated and realigned. But, in essence, hip hop music and street culture represented resistance to the patronizing interference of white supremacy and untenable Eurocentric norms and values imposed on us. This resistance and these possibilities were essential to the lure of the streets and hip hop culture. This perspective of hip hop is critical; it is either misunderstood, or erased, but in either case it is a lost perspective that needs to be reignited.

The longing for Black independence is historical and manifests and is expressed differently with each generation. As for the first generation of Blacks post-civil rights, we were unwilling to conform to whiteness and Eurocentric expectations. This unwillingness was expressed by hip-hop culture and the music explosion, particularly in the '70s through the '90s. Surviving and navigating the streets was synonymous with danger. But so was simply being Black in the US. The streets was the underground. A place rooted in possibilities for true Black liberation. A refuge for Black people living on their own terms, refusing to live by foreign norms or norms that fail to resonate with being Black.

The elders and the up-South generation were forced to watch from the windows of the businesses and companies that they had worked hard to bolster and enrich. They watched as crafts and trades that they learned—and others that they reinvented and perfected—didn't get handed down. As generational wealth declined to descend, they watched as branches were pruned from their family trees as easily as a gunshot to the head or a drug overdose. Of course they were disappointed, but they also understood that the vehicle that brought them there stalled on us and eventually became obsolete. What vehicle? Those manufacturing jobs. The vehicle that took our ancestors out of the Jim Crow South away from poverty, debt-peonage, and sharecropping and brought them into the middle and upper-middle classes. That vehicle was disassembled and discontinued; this is what deindustrialization represented to us. By the time I came of age, most of those factory buildings were broken glass, chained up, and abandoned relics.

So what was the inheritance for Generation X; the first free generation of Blackamericans born with all of the rights of US citizens? Why were no reparations or any sort of economic recovery mandated along with civil rights legislation? This historical context, like so much of the Black experience in the US, is undermined. Even more undermined was the white backlash that followed the passage of civil rights legislation. As historian Carol Anderson and many other US historians reminds us, every instance of Black progress in US history was met with a powerful and repressive backlash that Anderson called *White Rage*. The white backlash that our generation underwent was deindustrialization, economic divestment in our communities—art and enrichment programs were defunded and gutted, as pathways for tons of internationally grown cocaine flooded our cities and communities producing a market of death not seen in the history of post-enslavement America. The disease of addiction created a new economy, reflective of and driven by the same capitalistic market principles of greed that drove enslavement. Blackamerica seemed to change forever.

We were faced with every conceivable and inconceivable obstacle from enemies undeclared and unknown, we were conspired against, scapegoated, and deemed the root of America's problems, the source of her debauchery; and labeled America's *superpredators*. As a result, the occupation of our communities and the hunt for our bodies intensified.

White Rage and the Backlash of Civil Rights

Black communities and neighborhoods like ours in Waterbury, nationwide, from coast to coast, north to south were flooded with cocaine. Cocaine is a foreign substance neither grown nor produced anywhere in the United States. Who and what entities orchestrated and conducted the sophisticated, multi-billion dollar industry's transnational logistics necessary to cross the borders of the most powerful nation on earth? And who provided the geographical blueprints and maps to America's most vulnerable cities, communities, and neighborhoods occupied overwhelmingly by Blackamericans? Honest answers to these questions without historicizing the legacy of COINTELPRO cannot be taken seriously.

The crack phenomenon became an epidemic around the mid-1980s, and by the time I had entered high school in 1987–88 it was out of control. Our neighborhood ladies and gentleman, the pretty girls, and the fly guys were all of a sudden trapped in an unknowable topspin from experimenting with the drug. In our community, crack became a double-edged sword: on one end, fierce addiction, and the other, an insatiable economy. Millions of dollars in opportunities to sell drugs became the most attractive option unless you were an exceptional athlete. And frankly, despite all of the talent that came through, Waterbury did not have a reputation for producing professional athletes, with few exceptions.

In my freshman year at Wilby, I learned to navigate all of Waterbury's sociocultural, sociopolitical, and socioeconomic complexities. My introduction into early manhood came with limited choices: one was to focus on what my basketball coach offered. Basketball proved to be only a temporary escape, but it provided profound foundational lessons.

****

Hoop Dreams Above the Rim

Wilby basketball and Coach Reggie O'Brien gave me an opportunity and a platform that resulted in travel and state-wide media exposure. Basketball gave me confidence and fueled my aspirations of going to college. Although I didn't have aspirations to play in college or professionally, basketball helped me build strong ties in the state and opened up other possibilities across the region.

It would have been different had I been a 6'5"-plus, uber-talented dominant baller with skills like Phil Lott, but I wasn't on that level. Even though I exceeded expectations, I made All-State, won league and city championships, scored over 1,000 points, had a couple of respectable state-tourney runs, but I wasn't exceptional enough to make a living playing basketball and was more focused on other things. I wanted an HBCU experience, and that became my focus.

However, before graduation and the start of college, I had to overcome another self-constructed obstacle or setback during these pivotal high school years. Instead of four years, it took me five years to graduate because I had to repeat my second year for missing too many school days. I was in the street hustling my sophomore year and rarely attended school; I also did not play basketball that year. Consequently, I spent the summer after my sophomore year at MYI. There was a silver lining in all of this. MYI made me refocus on basketball, school, and I excelled academically my last two years. However, college recruitment was lukewarm. Even though I was getting straight As, colleges were not responding, and I didn't know why. I later realized the impact of school tracking. At Wilby, I was not tracked as gifted or cited for college prep courses. The curriculum wasn't preparing us and wasn't an appropriate bridge to college. So I was locked into non-college prep courses and a watered-down curriculum, and I didn't even know. I'm getting all As, not realizing that these grades were not setting me up for my future. I finally dedicated myself to doing well

72

academically, but I wasn't getting the kinds of responses from colleges and universities that I'd hoped for.

The majority of students at Wilby were Black and Puerto Rican. The school brought together a colorful collective of kids of various Black Caribbean and Cape Verdean families; similarly, the white kids represented various European ethnicities: Italian, Irish, Portuguese, the Balkans, and Jewish people from different Eastern and Southern European countries. It was less prohibited in Waterbury than other places in the US for us to hang-out in each other's homes and eat together. It was a unique melting pot in this regard, though not perfect; extraordinarily unique is what I would come to know as I got older, traveled, and met people from other cities across the US. Some of this could be attributed to the power of sports in a sense. Despite these notable exceptions, the racism and White supremacy was very real in Waterbury.

Yet there were only four Black teachers at Wilby; two taught gym. A third was the history teacher, who miraculously also taught us Black history—hands down the best classes I had in my whole K-12 experience. The fourth Black teacher was Mr. Jenkins, the math teacher. Although I never had him, he was docile; and that stood out. I could not relate to his characteristics, which contrasted the strong Black men in my life. He was a pushover, and Wilby was the wrong stage for pushovers. So four Black teachers in the whole school—and the only man, spineless—yet the women, conversely, were strong like the ones in my family. They reflected the dignity and strength of my aunts, and we respected that because we were familiar with their qualities. Unfortunately, however, my high school guidance counselor, who had predicted my demise by the age of 21, was also a Black woman.

In Mrs. Norman's African history course, she shared her personal experiences on a trip to Egypt. She taught us about the Nubian people, their history, and their contributions to ancient Egypt and civilization. She returned from Egypt with photos and videos that she had filmed and these provided important context related to her teachings about the Nubians in Egypt, Africa. Everyone in that class was engaged, including the white, the Puerto Rican, and of course the Black kids. Years later, as adults my classmates would still talk about how memorable those lessons were. The early 1990s introduced me to Brand Nubians, a popular rap group. They made socially and politically conscious hip hop music, and it was the first time the term *Nubian* reached my consciousness. I assumed it just meant African people in general. I did not know it was a specific tribe of powerful and ancient Africans that ruled and inhabited what is today known as Egypt. Today, I marvel at what Mrs. Norman exposed me to—something that I could not have known—my destiny.

The Black women gym teachers put together an annual HBCU trip for two weeks and would escort us on a visit to several HBCUs along the coast, down south, and back up. I had evolved by then, changed from the knucklehead that I was in my first two years at Wilby. Based on my behavior early on, they would not have approved of me going on that HBCU trip. But by the time my senior year came around, I had built relationships with them, and they trusted me as much as I respected them.

74

So when it was time for that trip, I asked if I could go, and they replied, "Absolutely, you can go, and you should go."

That trip changed my life. We went to Delaware State, then we drove down to Lincoln in Pennsylvania, on to Maryland and both Bowie and Morgan State, then down to Virginia, to Virginia Union in Richmond and Virginia State in Petersburg, then Norfolk State and Hampton. Even as far as North Carolina to North Carolina Central, NC A&T, Shaw, and UNC-Chapel Hill, even though it wasn't an HBCU. Highlights were Norfolk State University and Howard in DC, of course. The HBCU experience opened my eyes, and I went home thinking, "Oh shit, I'm going to an HBCU!" I applied to all of them, and the only one that accepted me was Virginia State University in Petersburg, Virginia, where I eventually went.

That's the clean version. There was still trouble, violence, temptations, and trip-ups that kept me tumbling toward a fall no matter how high I thought I had reached. This dichotomy followed me around for many years. The life I wanted to live and the life that I inherited, the people, and lifelong bonds seemed to pull me in different directions.

Prelude to a Dark Rite of Passage

The lessons I learned in the streets were too many to count. These lessons were a mixed bag of a lot of good and bad. One thing was certain: the streets were not for the faint of heart. And from my standpoint it is where the most revolutionary-minded Blackamericans found comfort and shelter. Your rites of passage come from knowing how and when to fight. You have to be fearless and wise in order to navigate and survive. Regardless of your level of fearlessness and heart, being foolish and not moving wisely could cost your life. I reflect mostly on the good in retrospect as an adult, because much of the bad I have, perhaps unconsciously, tried to forget.

The survival skills that I learned at a young age still resonate and I rely on and trust them even today. The streets provided an extra sensory perception necessary for survival. Survival included eluding police who controlled and patrolled Black communities like an occupational force.

Our local policemen were often strangers from suburban towns with no connection and no respect for the communities and the people who lived there. There were exceptions as some of the Black and Puerto Rican cops and a few white cops that lived and went to school in the city, and played sports with guys from there, were at times more compassionate and empathetic. Other times they were just as oppressive and even more so than the white suburban cops who misunderstood, or straight-up hated us.

Also, the crack epidemic and the new economy manufactured new enemies and festered divisions between our communities and families. The competition for drugs and drug territory where lots of money was to be made caused deadly turf wars that tore apart kinships.

The streets engulfed much of our family who were born and raised up north. Although our ancestors relocated from Franklin County, North Carolina for a better life—trailing the legacy of enslavement—they found the family tree splintering from the lure of the streets.

The negative connotation to the streets is well deserved. But there were other aspects and valuable codes. Such as integrity, loyalty and being recognized as a man/woman of your word. Be straight up or risk getting labeled distrustful and shady. These values I took with me as I transitioned from the streets into my academic life where I learned many of these values and codes did not exist. In the academy I have experienced levels of untrustworthiness, disloyalty, and predatory behavior that will shame some of the worst qualities I had encountered in the streets. Not surprisingly, these traits extend to the corporate and political arenas as well.

Despite the deadly street-life that we signed up for, there was never a shortage of fun, joy, and laughter among cousins and the kids from our neighborhoods. And as for the hustling that it eventually evolved into, it stemmed from choosing to eat and provide for loved ones or not. It does not matter whether you agree or understand it, these were the bare-boned facts. And this is why many of us, knowing the risks—prison and death— nearly everyone was willing to take it. We were not crazy predators, we were

77

just looking for a way out. It's easy to look at our situation in a vacuum. But the reality is what we experienced was the inheritance of a legacy, centuries of systemic oppression, repression, and divestment.

Despite these conditions, we recognized each other's humanity through a shared pain or comradery from brotherhood found in prison. Like the laughter that quickly returned to us just moments after funerals. Through centuries of pain, death and lying about it in plain sight, we found and established tribes, people worth fighting with and for, and the people worth loving and crying with.

All that said, and with no further preamble, I bare as much as I dare of my unglorified experiences in those streets. Hardcore tales that could have taken this storyteller long before I could become a man.

CHAPTER FIVE
Street Dreams Are Made of These

I was in Harlem one winter around 1990. Harlem was our plug. *Papi* was there along with all of the wholesale cocaine money could buy. And here I was 17 years old, having made this trip hundreds of times already for the past 2 to 3 years, and seemingly out of nowhere, a guy stood 10 inches from my face, with his gun poking my ribs. "Gimme your money!" It happened so suddenly that it left me frozen.

I tried to stall him, "Yo, hold up . . . ," but he wasn't there to talk, so I went in my pants pocket, where I had about $200 cash. I had on a puffy, goose-down winter coat with a few thousand dollar stacks zipped up in an inside pocket. He quickly snatched the couple hundred from my hand and said, "Give me your coat." Damn. That's ALL my money. I can't give it up. I spent some cold winter nights and risked my freedom on some of Waterbury's hottest blocks. And just like that give it up? Fuck that!

He said, "Take off your coat . . . ." I could comply or risk getting shot. My partner, who had taken the trip with me, stood there frozen like a deer in headlights. The only weapon among us was poking me in my ribs. Understanding street life is knowing that the streets don't lose nor do they change, and you'd better figure out another method. And navigating the streets takes wisdom. My jacket and all the money I had to my name were taken that day. The streets were cold.

I almost died in Harlem. I have an estranged relationship with Harlem. It's where my missing biological father was born and was killed. It is where my grandfather Sonny-Man ended up relocating and where he was found dead. But Harlem sparred my life. I remember the look in the man's eyes; he was an older Black dude who did not seem cold nor like a killer. However, he was a professional stickup kid who thought enough to spare my life. He must've been in his early to mid-thirties. I wonder what he thought of me. I was not some big kid as a teenager. I had a baby face and was probably 140 pounds soaking wet. It was a close call—one among many that proceeded it.

*****

Growing up in Waterbury, you earned respect by either being a gifted athlete, a witty smooth talker, a comedian, or you had a fighting/boxing pedigree. I learned that lesson as early as eight years old with a kid named Ragar Overstreet (Ray). I met Ragar when I was in third grade, after we'd moved from the Sugar Bowl area to Bishop Street across the street from the magical Fulton Park. Ray lived on Bishop Street a few houses down from me. And being that I was new to the neighborhood, I was tested on sight. Ray, his siblings, and all the neighborhood kids would surround and interrogate me whenever I passed by his house. They never jumped on me, but they could have. I had to tell someone in my family because they were deep and terrifying. One day, my Cousin Derreck walked home with me and when we got close to Ray's house, I chose to go down a side street to avoid them.

The Color of Sun Ray's: Ragar Overstreet and Facing Fear

My cousin stopped me and asked, "Where are you going?" I told him I just wanted to go a different way home to avoid Ragar and his crew. I was around 8 years old and Derreck was 11. Unfazed he looked at me and said, "Nah, we going *this* way." I turned around and faced my fears and walked up Bishop with someone older and braver than me leading the way. In hindsight, that's how I navigated the streets as a young kid, following in the footsteps of those who walked the path already, those who assured me of the way. Being afraid was part of the journey. The lesson is in what you do with that fear. Do you face those fears or retreat?

As soon as we got by Ray's house, sure enough he jumped off the porch and began interrogating me. Me and Derreck were outnumbered, but my cousin was not scared and I was calmed by that. At the time I didn't know it, but Ray was only three years older than me. Under his interrogations, though, it felt like he was around 20 years old. Even then, he was a tall, light-complexioned brother with a big frame that was already hardened by life's circumstances.

I remember going home crying and looking for some comfort from my mother after those initial confrontations with Ray. Instead, she yelled at me, "Why the hell are you crying?" I told her about the kids down the street and what had happened. She, I realized later, understood that it would keep happening if I did not defend myself. She yelled at me and insisted that I fight and defend myself.

I recall grabbing this big-ass pole that was in our pantry, it looked like one of those long 6- or 7-foot poles you saw in old Kung Fu movies. I have no idea why this pole was in our house, I just grabbed it and charged out the door, but before I could take two steps my mom snatched it from my hand and redirected me back to our kitchen.

There were relatively no more harassments that I can think of for a time until later that summer at the Pearl Street Summer Camp at what we called, The "Q." There, many of my cousins were either workers at the camp or campers. Ragar was a camper alongside me and some of his older family members as well. Once my family found out what happened with Ray and I, it was arranged for us to fight it out one-on-one in the park.

Even though Ragar was much bigger and more hardened than I was and older than me by three years, I had to make my stand or there would never be peace. Somehow at age eight, I understood this. Everything up until that point told me that fighting him was a mismatch. But having all of my cousins there gave me confidence. This was a feeling I would later become used to as I got older and navigated the North End of the city.

The circle was drawn and Ragar and I fought. I more than held my own and I think it was established in that moment that I had what it took to not have to live my life terrified of the inevitable challenges of growing up in the North End.

Immediately after the fight, on our way back to The "Q" from the park, Ray and I instantly bonded. In many respects that fight validated me. He and I became inseparable. He walked alongside me that day and stopped, made a muscle, and told me to feel his bicep. Nothing odd for 8–11-year-olds coming of age. It was his extension of his friendship to me. He turned out to be one of my best and closest friends from that moment into the next 11 years.

A few days before I left for college, some of my old friends were hanging out on The Bowl. Ragar was one of them . . . a fight broke out on this particular day and someone ended up in the hospital in bad shape. I remember Ray yelling at me and chastising me because, in a few days, I was leaving the city for Virginia State University. This was the summer of 1992 after I had graduated high school. Some of my friends were excited about it although far less interested in that path for themselves because they were more captivated by all the money opportunities that the streets offered. Still, they were happy for me. Ray was yelling at me that day for a reason. I am only left to speculate what that reason was. Perhaps he saw in me something bigger than what the streets offered?

The day I was leaving for VSU, I saw him near downtown, so I pulled over and picked him up. We talked, listened to music, laughed and joked as we'd done for over a decade. He was a funny, over-the-top hilarious dude. I dropped him off and went back to packing and loading our van for the college drop-off. A couple of weeks into my first semester at VSU, I received a call that Ray had been shot five times in the chest and died. The heartbreak is still as unimaginable today as when I heard it that day. I heard all of the stories and what had happened. The truth of the matter is, Ray was the toughest, hardest kid in my generation. He would fight anyone and could beat most everyone that he did. Even if he couldn't beat them, he was unafraid to find out. I saw him fight some of the most epic one-on-ones against older guys and against bigger odds, so his reputation was solid. The guy who shot Ray understood that he didn't stand a chance in a head-up fight, and so he shot Ray. Took him away from his parents, many sisters, brothers, nieces and nephews, his children, and many of his friends like me. Ray was taken away from us at the tender age of 22. The first fight I ever had was with Ray, and he was also one of the unfortunate first examples of how the odds had increased from the prowess of the hands to the power of the gun.

*****

The Heat of Summer in Dirty Water

I'd just finished my freshman year at Wilby and summers in Waterbury were live growing up. I had friends and family all over the city and therefore access to all the live neighborhoods. Violence was everywhere growing up, but there were degrees to it.

The summer of 1988, after my freshman year at Wilby I was visiting some of my friends from rival Crosby High School up in the Long Hill housing projects—LHP, or notoriously known as "The Hill." I was there, sitting outside of the community center across the street from the main entrance to the projects. I crossed the street to go check on one of my friends and upon returning back to the community center I bumped into Melle B., or Mell-Mell, who was coming into the projects as I was leaving.

He was two days away from turning 20, and I was 15 years old. He was the same age as most of my heroes at the time, like my Cousins Ree and Jake . . . they were all in the same age range . . . so young but the reflection of grown men to me. In any case, Melle B he lived on The Bowl back in the day and much like my cousins was someone who I revered. They played hoops in his yard, while I would stay on the sidelines and watch from this huge fence he had in his yard. I once fell from that fence and split open my head. That fall required six stitches to close a gash over my left eye. I must have been about 10 years old. My cousins walked me back to my grandmother's house that day, about a 10-minute walk, putting pressure on my gushing face all the way.

Fast-forward several years later, Melle B. and I locked eyes that day in front of the projects in an old and familiar brotherhood. His footsteps were worth following. He had been the starting point guard on Wilby's basketball team two years prior. We spoke and caught up briefly, exchanged good luck wishes and dap before I rejoined my friends. I was feeling good about myself, the summer and life and coming of age at a time ripe with much possibility.

Shortly after this interaction we heard a commotion, saw people running through the projects, followed by sirens and screaming. Not knowing what was happening, we jumped up off of our stoops and followed the crowd to the basketball court where people were huddled and looking down at the ground. I pushed my way through the crowd and ended up standing next to my Cousin Tra Mack's old girlfriend, a fly girl named Michelle. She was in shock with her hand over her mouth looking at the person laying on the ground. I looked down, but could not recognize the person laying two feet away from me. I looked around and everyone seemed to identify this person and so I refocused and looked again but I still could not make him out. His eyes were open and he had on a ring that kept sparkling in the summer sunlight, which rather than be beautiful, was like a warning flash.

I asked Michelle "Who is he?" She replied without looking at me, "It's Mell-Mell." I was shocked! I couldn't register that the young man I had just spoken to not even 15 minutes prior was now laying lifeless in a pool of blood. I do not know who killed Mell-Mell or why. But Waterbury had become a destination for NYC drug dealers and tensions over drug turf were about to boil over. As a result, fights and shootings were frequent. I had never witnessed anything like what happened to Mell. His death was the gateway to understanding what the new crack economy had in store for us. These years coincide with my own deep engagement with the lure of the streets and hustling.

The Bowl: The Building Where Life Started and Almost Ended
As the drug market bloomed, the Sugar Bowl became ground zero. My earliest involvement with drugs and the streets intensified on the block where I was born, and my life almost ended right there on that very same

86

corner. One summer afternoon at The Bowl, words were exchanged and a confrontation happened with a guy from out of town. He was sent home embarrassed. Hours later, after sundown, he came back. I was sitting on the stoop of the Sugar Bowl talking to a couple of my home girls when I noticed someone about a football field away. His head was on a swivel and he was walking fast up North Main Street toward The Bowl. The girls were talking, not noticing what I was noticing as he got closer. Tracking his moves, he was clearly looking for someone. As he got closer, I recognized it was the dude from out of town who we sent home embarrassed earlier, and as I noticed him he noticed me at the same time. He started running toward me and reaching for his gun. Stalled by having to cross busy North Main Street traffic, I was able to run along the side of the Sugar Bowl building as he started shooting.

He continued shooting as I ran run up the stairs. I knew the building, having been born in and raised there for many years. I banged on the first-floor door after climbing about 40 flights of stairs. Luckily someone opened the back door and I darted through the long hallway in the building to the front door. I ran down the stairs which took me to another street, which was next to a bar where my cousins hung out. I saw my two cousins, Stevie and Reese, who were with some of their boys. I told them a kid from out of town was shooting at me. They went into war mode. As I began describing him they identified him, his local girlfriend, where she lived and where they hung out. Not even 10 minutes later we were two car loads deep making the rounds to find him.

We got in the car and headed to their hangout—he wasn't there and his girl had just left, we were told. So we returned to the cars and drove toward where his girl lived. We found him walking along the way headed in the direction of his girl's house. I won't say more except that the next day one of the local Black detectives stopped by to ask if I had anything to do with a shooting. Of course I acted like I had no clue what he was talking about. Just another day for me coming of age in Waterbury.

*****

The Afro-Latino Festival

Brawls between New Yorkers and other guys from out of town had become normal. I had been in several of these brawls from a young age. I sat front row for one of the most legendary brawls that was talked about for many years. It occurred in the summer of 1989 at 16 years old during the annual Afro-Latino festival, a celebration of Black and Puerto Rican culture and food. That year the festival was overrun by New Yorkers and tensions were higher than ever. The guys from New York were easy to spot and there were a lot of them. They were flexing hard and they were deep. But some of Waterbury's most thorough and rugged young men and notorious crews were there and more kept coming and a standoff ensued. And right in the middle of it all, my Cousin Reese broke ranks, zeroed in on one of their front liners and chaos erupted. The festival was held on a gravel parking lot near downtown between the North Square Projects and the

North Square Park. As the brawl escalated, crowds of people began to run and clouds of dust made it hard to see. The scene was chaos.

Life as we knew it was changing right before our eyes. The new crack economy had consumed all of us and altered the DNA of our communities and culture. The guys from NYC were our brothers. All of them had the same migration story and pathways from the South as we did. Many of their elders and our elders were relatives or neighbors in the Jim Crow counties and cities from where they had fled. The Southern values instilled in us were being traded for dollars. And in order to get those dollars your mindset had to shift. And given most of our socioeconomic status, most of us did not see this shift as a bad exchange.

*****

Brothers Become Enemies and Brothers Again

In the following summer of 1990 at age 17, in that same North Square Park, I was with some older cousins hustling the graveyard shift, the hours after 11:00 pm usually until sunrise. I still have a Polaroid from that day with the date and time scribbled on it. After staying in the park all night a few of us walked to the Sugar Bowl to get breakfast. Shortly after, someone who had just left the park came in the restaurant and told us someone was just shot in the park. We all started looking around thinking about who we left there. That night/morning it was myself my older Cousins C-Dale, Reese, and D-Pruden. We were all accounted for. Later we learned that someone from the neighborhood in the park with us had shot one of the guys from NY in the back of the head. Luckily Raheem, who was from Queens, managed to survive. We all knew Raheem; I was involved with some other guys who had clashed with him previously. He was a reputable guy who commanded respect who could be seen walking through the city alone. But this day he barely escaped with his life. Years would pass before I heard or saw Raheem again.

Maybe 17 years later I ran into Raheem and happened to stand behind him in line at a local pizza spot in Waterbury. I knew him right away. He was still the same tall, light-skinned, swagged out dude whose path I crossed as a young teenager. Before he could turn around I studied the bullet wound in the back of his bald head while he ordered his food. I wondered to myself . . . *Damn. How much does he remembered me or know of my old association with the people and events that led to his shooting?* He turned around and was surprisingly really friendly, a subtle smile and head nod of acknowledgment or familiarity. I hadn't been in Waterbury for a while, and I had just returned after living in Atlanta for a decade. Perhaps overly cautious, I returned the gesture as he turned around and sat down with his food.

While I was doing my bid in Georgia, Raheem was doing his own prison term in Connecticut. When the New York guys did bids in CT, often bonds formed that sometimes squashed former street altercations. By the time our paths crossed again in the pizza shop, he and I both were Muslims. I started bumping into him at the local mosques and eventually we became friends and brothers. I'd met his family—his mom and kids, and he'd met mine. Everyone in the city knew who had shot Raheem and I am sure he knew as well. But it never came up in any of our conversations, but he told me about the banging migraines he suffered due to the bullet still lodged in his head.

Through it all, Raheem was a solid, stand-up dude who maintained his fiery, warrior spirit but he definitely had matured and evolved. He was a family man, with a wife and kids. He was still a hustler, albeit a different type with several entrepreneurial projects and streams of income. I was proud of him.

"Connecticut took a lot of years from me. Prison, getting shot . . . all that. I'm done with that past," he explained. I was looking at a man who in those dark street interludes represented the best of us who had survived. Most of who we described as the most thorough guys, with mentalities of warriors and soldiers, did not make it. But if you survived, you carried the scars that show the many ways you could have died—like Raheem.

*****

The Day That Love Died

After Virginia State, and just before I moved to Atlanta, I had one street interlude that scarred me deeper than anything up until that point. Or maybe it was a culmination of tragedies and scars that had piled up? I don't know, but I had definitely reached a breaking point. This tragedy involved one of the most precious and influential young men who I ever personally

91

knew at that point in my life. His name was Christopher Blake Love, affectionally known in Waterbury as C-Love. C-Love grew up around us in the North Square Projects close to downtown. But unlike so many of us, he avoided street life and went the path of academia. He was six years older than me, a mentor, and one of the city's rarest and most precious gems. Chris was a well-known and respected high school basketball player. After high school, he went to Hampton the HBCU in VA, but transferred to play college hoops for a Division III basketball program. From there he went on to the University of Fairfield for his Master's degree and eventually enrolled in the University of Rhode Island's PhD program in Applied Psychology.

When I was still in high school, Chris went out of his way to find me whenever he came to Waterbury. I was a Sugar Bowl regular, the livest and hottest block in the city, easy to find. He would whip his Carolina Blue Volkswagen Jetta to the curb and hop out once he spotted me. C-Love was fly, unique, special, and always sharp; sometimes dressed in suspenders and a tie and sometimes just casual. We would dap and embrace and he'd ask what I was doing and if I wanted to ride with him. I always obliged. We'd ride and he'd ask me about school and my future plans. He always encouraged and talked to me respectfully, as if I were a peer.

He founded a local newspaper called *Da Ghetto*, what translated today would be a podcast or a blog. His work and his thoughts on the state of Blackamericans was critical, historical, unique, and well-received. To say that he was the epitome of his name—Love—well-loved and respected was an understatement.

On Halloween night in 1993, C-Love held a fundraiser and a party for *Da Ghetto* in Waterbury at a local spot in the North End near The Bowl. C-Love and his presence usually brought out the classiest, most talented, and level headed people in Waterbury, and surrounding areas of different ethnicities, cultures and backgrounds. By all accounts it was a positive night. And as people started leaving and saying goodbyes, a couple of loose cannons from around the North End came. I was not there, but I was told from those who were there that an argument started because the food was gone. This led to one of the guys, who we all knew, pulling out a gun and after a few words at Chris squeezed the trigger. Chris was shot at pointblank range in the eye and subsequently passed away.

For years, I grappled with the question of who would/could kill someone so loved? Particularly, who from amongst us, the inner-city neighborhoods in Waterbury? Chris was ONLY known as an intelligent Black man who loved Black people, and lived his life striving to be an academic in the service of Black people. The US has no clue what it lost. Deep in the weeds of the statistically worst metropolitan city in the country, in its roughest neighborhood, the brightest of gems was stolen away.

The next morning, my Cousin Stevie and Ann, his girlfriend at the time, came to my house. Ann asked me if I heard about what had happened the night before. Of course I hadn't. This was the era before cell phones and social media. She described the story just mentioned. When she told me who the shooter was, I was shocked and overcome with grief and disbelief. I could not even find the correlation between the two. The shooter, although he came from a well-respected and classy family, he was the black sheep and a wild-card. He had done multiple prison stints, was known to kick up dust, and bust his gun.

Chris was just the opposite—he was no threat, never known to carry a gun. Or involved in anything that required that. We were all from North End. Our families and communities were all interrelated and connected. There should have been no beef deep enough for someone so promising to die so senselessly. In the promised land of Waterbury, CT. The land our families migrated to from the vestiges of enslavement and vice grips of Jim Crow hoping for a better future for their future generations—us. And here we were.

After Chris' senseless killing, I hated Waterbury, and the mindset that it cultivated in so many of us who grew up there. I remember thinking if Chris' life had no value in Waterbury, then I didn't stand a chance. At that time I was running the streets heavy. Involved with anything you could think. C-Love died on Halloween and by Thanksgiving, I was in Atlanta visiting my homeboy who had left Waterbury a few years prior. By December, I had packed up my apartment in Bucks Hill and relocated to Atlanta. In hindsight, moving to Atlanta was meant to be a fresh start. A breath of much-needed fresh air needed after every time I'd had it knocked out of me in a street fight, or from the of shock standing over a friend's corpse, or in breathless disbelief of another valuable life I cherished stolen away.

Although the death of C-Love was not something that the nation grieved, but rest assured every Black and Brown person and many white folks in the city and surrounding areas who knew him and came to know him posthumously were crushed. The devastation and grief was palpable. I remember walking through the Waterbury mall to buy clothes for the funeral and every recognizable face who I saw had the same devastated expression. No words were needed.

Chris died in 1993 at age 26. And 26 years later, another vastly different yet eerily similar tragic murder occurred. On March 31, 2019, which would have been C-Love's 52nd birthday, Nipsey Hussle was shot and killed in his own neighborhood in Los Angeles, amongst his own people. Ironically, I was living in Southern California when Nipsey died, and even though his music did not shape my coming of age in the ways Biggie and Pac did, I was more devastated at the loss of Nipsey. It wasn't until much later did I realize the many connections between Chris and Nipsey, as vastly different as they were on the surface. They were both unapologetic in their love for Black people, loved their communities and strived for excellence. They both reached their paths through different means yet tragically died the same way, in the place and amongst the people who they loved most and fought the hardest for. What many in the nation, including me, felt when Nipsey died accurately depicts C-Love's murder for those of us who knew him.

CHAPTER SIX
Off the Block and On to College

Prior to the murder of Chris love, I had a short-lived HBCU experience at Virginia State University (VSU). I enrolled at VSU in the fall of 1992. VSU was approximately a seven-hour drive from Waterbury to Petersburg, Virginia, about one hour from Richmond. I went away to college hoping for a fresh start and to get away from the omnipresent dark choices and opportunities all around me in Waterbury. VSU enlightened me regarding many of my peers throughout the cities on the East Coast who were experiencing the same tragedies and looking for similar escape routes as me. What had also become clear was the vast gap between the poor *education* offered to me by Waterbury public and parochial schools, and the expectations of college life. I was not prepared.

At VSU I attracted and bonded with those familiar with the street life, either themselves or through family members and loved ones. Mainly those from the tri-state region, New York, New Jersey, and Connecticut. And others who at the time I knew very little about, such as my peers from the DC, Maryland, and Virginia (DMV) areas. While in VA it had also been made clear that the once-burgeoning crack economy had become a well-oiled machine. The devalue of precious Black life required to succeed in this

96

new economy was hitting on all cylinders and spreading across multiple regions.

The city of Richmond, just up the road from VSU, was as dangerous as any place I knew or heard about. The local Richmond radio stations were reporting new homicides daily. During my time at VSU, Richmond held the unfortunate moniker as the US murder capital. Gun violence and homicide was off the charts. Having lived in the not-so-distant shadows of NYC and in some of the most divested and underserved cities in Southern Connecticut, I was no stranger to the violence and the entrapments that the new economy created. However, just as no one would think to associate it with CT, I was unaware of what was happening in Virginia. VSU had opened my mind in so many ways, the least of which was academically.

Nonetheless, the all-Black academic environment was a comforting experience, and, except for my trips to Harlem to shop, cop, or kick it growing up, I had not seen such a concentration of Black people before in my life. Plus these were my peers from different walks of life, and various cities across the US. But we were 18–20-year-old kids, many of us struggling to break from the common urban mischief toward a better life. Like me, many still carried the stench of the streets, and like me, were still inclined and able to set it off if cornered.

College *is* a War Zone

My most memorable VSU moments did not involve book learning. Instead, the very familiar patterns of violence centered around some method to get money. Like the death of Sonnet, a senior at VSU who was well-liked and admired. I first came in contact with him over the summer during incoming freshman orientation. He was an upperclassman who I had very little interaction with, but he stood out to me during orientation. A tall, brown-skinned brother cool and respectable, who gave off Chris Love vibes.

I saw him sporadically around campus and we would greet each other with the standard show of respect head nod. One weekend after returning from Norfolk, VA, where I visited frequently because a large concentration of friends from Waterbury went to Norfolk State and nearby Hampton University. I stopped by my close friend's apartment, a fellow freshman from NYC, but he wasn't home. One of his friends, also part of our freshman class, answered the door. I will refer to this guy as Killer. Killer opened the door and let me in and I waited around for our mutual friend to come home. While waiting the news came on TV and teased a news story about the murder of VSU students and promptly cut to commercial. My mind started to race, I took quick inventory of the freshman class that I came in with. This was a wild bunch and something in my gut was signaling something.

After the commercial break and a few other stories less important to me, the story resumed. Two roommates, VSU seniors, were victims of a home invasion and murdered execution style. Found duct taped and shot at

98

close range. When they mentioned the names of the victims I was stunned—one of whom was Sonnet. There were no arrests made and no suspects at that time. My jaw dropped and I yelled out, "Yo, can you believe this shit? Who would want to kill Sonnet, he was such a cool dude?" Killer was pacing around the house, cleaning, packing and moving around nervously. "Yeah, that's wild, that's fucked up . . ." he said. Less impacted I guess because he was not at orientation with us and probably just didn't know him, I thought. I waited for a while longer for our mutual friend to return, still in a haze of disbelief at the news of Sonnet. Finally, I told Killer to tell our friend that I stopped by and that I would see him another time.

A few days later, news was announced regarding the double homicide of the two VSU seniors. Sonnet and his roommate's murderers were apprehended. The local news reported the arrest of several of my fellow freshmen classmen who were charged with the murders. One of the trigger men was the guy I called Killer, who I had sat with at our mutual friend's house. I sat there interacting with him with no clue of the blood on his hands. Killer and I were not friends. We had a few mutual associates. But my street instincts alerted me to keep my distance. But even my worst suspicions regarding him did not see him doing something like that. I never learned the name of Sonnet's roommate and did not know him. But my sincere condolences go out to both of the families for their tragic losses.

I recall hearing stories about the lynch mob crew from NYC on campus at VSU. They were an ominous crew of upperclassmen from the East Coast. The ones who I met were fifth- or sixth-year seniors from

Mount Vernon, Brooklyn, and Queens. They were much older and more mature than I was. I met them in the weight room while working out and they pulled me into their circle and showed me love. I began working out with three of them on a regular basis. They pushed me in the weight room and held me down around campus. I bonded with one in particular, Kareem from Brooklyn. He had a girlfriend in Richmond and would come and get me on campus and take me on the ride from Petersburg to Richmond periodically. We would chop it up on the ride about life, about school, the state of the world or whatever. It was like a big brother relationship, a closeness that I felt with some of my older cousins growing up in Waterbury. I appreciated and valued Kareem.

A Historical Beautiful Oasis of Blackness and Potential

While at VSU I was introduced to the DC go-go music scene, the dances and frenzy that came with it. DJ Kool used to DJ our Gym-Jams and the beautiful girls from the DMV (Washington, DC/Maryland/Virginia) area would do their line-dance all across the gym. While we came to VSU from cities that were close regionally, East Coast Black cultures are diverse even though we all sprouted from the same Southern roots. It was a world different from mine, but the Blackness was all the same and quite familiar.

I met Jason Swain from the Bronx who became a lifelong friend. Swain was cool, dresses fly and had easy to vibe with mannerisms. He reminded me of some of the fly dudes from Waterbury who I grew up with. Swain and I became friends almost instantly. We both left VSU after one year—I went back to CT and he returned to NYC—but we kept in contact.

It was shortly after I had left VSU when C-Love died. And as I mentioned, two months later I moved to Atlanta. Swain came to visit me during Freaknik 1994, which prompted his move to Atlanta. We were roommates for a time. I admired Swain because he was one of the few people my age who knew exactly what he wanted to do. He wanted to write, produce, and direct films. And over the years he dedicated his life to his stories and filmmaking.

The beautiful sea of Black students at VSU was motivation to leave the harshness of Waterbury behind me. I had a map of Waterbury on my closet door in my dorm with certain streets highlighted as places where I did not want to be or return. I had to look at this map every time I walked in or out of my room. For the first time I had been away from home outside of the few months span (in the MYI Youth Correctional facilities), and it felt like I could re-write the negative script that was written for me.

At VSU I was understanding the commonalities between those of us from the Northeast cities and our kin who remained in the South. My HBCU experience was like a reintroduction to family members. The offspring of those who fled Jim Crow and those who rode it out and remained in the South. Yet here we were, discovering or rediscovering one another. Feelings of mutual love, respect, and kinship.

VSU was a way to escape Waterbury. It was difficult because up until that point the streets had influenced much of what I knew about life. And trouble was never far.

I was raised a hustler; it was in my DNA. My father was one and all of my older cousins were, too. And even though I was in college, I was still broke. I was watching all my friends buy weed, then I saw an opportunity, and remembered my friend from Waterbury—now living in the Norfolk Hampton area—was a weed connect. He was an upperclassmen at one of the HBCUs in that area, who used to get money back home, and took his hustle with him to Virginia. I called him up and told him what I needed and he said come through. In a short while many of my friends and associates at VSU began buying weed from me.

Grab the Weed and Jet

One day some of my friends from high school, who were attending Norfolk State, came to VSU for a basketball game. They came to my dorm room and asked if they could smoke weed in my dorm room. I had been in so many smoke sessions in the dorms and I thought I understood the science of how to keep the weed smoke from escaping into the dorm halls. The science involved an industrial-size fan, a wide open dorm room window and some towels under the door. I watched my peers do it all the time, and thought I understood and tried it that day. In hindsight, my idea was not very bright or maybe my execution was ineffective? Anyway, I left the fan on and we went to the basketball game on campus. After the game, before dropping me off and heading back to Norfolk, I noticed a cop car in front of my dorm hall. I said to my homeboy, "Don't leave yet. Let me see what this is about."

I left them sitting in the middle of the street, car running, as I went upstairs to my room. Sure enough a campus police officer was standing in front of my door. I'm thinking, "Damn! I've got weed in my closet." I played it off and walked past him down the hall to the bathroom. I looked in the mirror and asked myself, *What the fuck you gonna do?*

I walked back towards my room, and the cop was standing to the left side of the door. I walked past him nodded my head in acknowledgement and went to put my key in the door. He stopped me saying, "You can't go in." Acting surprised, I replied, "This is my room, what do you mean I can't go in?"

"This is your room?" he asked.

"Yeah," I answered, because what else?

"If you give me permission to search it, you can go in," he replied.

"Alright, you can search it," I agreed because I knew I had a lock on my closet. I opened the door and saw they had already been in and had ransacked my room; it was a mess, clothes were everywhere. But the lock was still on my closet.

I asked, "What is going on, who wrecked my room?"

He replied, "Marijuana was reported coming from your room so we entered and searched it, and we're waiting on a search warrant to pop your lock and search your closet"

I kept cool, as one of my friends who was waiting in the car showed up, looking worried. He asked, "You alright?"

"Yeah, man. I don't know what's up with these cops . . ." I turned to the cop and said, "I've got to give him something, they're about to leave town."

I popped my lock on my closet. There were two bags on the top shelf. One had shoes, and the other had the weed, which I was not about to hand over to the campus cop along with my freedom. I grabbed the bag with the shoes, and as I was handing it to my friend, the cop stopped me and said, "No, I have to search it first." I gave it to him and as he turned his attention to look through the bag, I snatched the bag with the weed and pushed past my friend and ran out, closing the door behind me. The cop followed behind me down the hall, down the stairs, and to my boy's car— still in the middle of the street with the engine running. I threw the bag in the car and yelled—"Jet!" And without hesitation, he jetted off in his triple-black Volkswagen Jetta. I tried obstructing the cop's view, who was behind me radioing in the license plate.

This incident happened long before cellphones, and it remains a mystery how my two friends reconnected. They were unfamiliar with the VSU campus yet somehow managed to reconnect and get off campus and onto the highway, and gone.

The cop had me in handcuffs sitting on the curb waiting for his backup and his superiors to arrive. A Black sheriff with a canine along with more cops returned. The sheriff was pissed off at me and let me know as he grilled me.

"What the fuck, what was in that bag? Who were those guys?" he asked. I'm sitting there looking stupid as hell, and not saying shit. They took

104

me to the campus police station and I sat there all night, with the sheriff interrogating me in vain, while I avoided and ignored his questions.

I sat looking at the clock, hoping my friends make it back to Norfolk. I remember thinking, *If I don't hear anything in two hours, the time to get from Petersburg to Norfolk, I'm going to sleep.* I was nervous but cool for two hours hoping the sheriff's scanner did not alert him that they found the car. The irony of it all; two Black men from two different generations diametrically opposed. What were basic survival skills for me had him clamoring to lock me up.

After about two or three hours, I kicked back thinking, "Hell, I'm going to sleep. They're gonna have to let me go tomorrow." Remarkably, when I woke up in the morning, the sheriff had not heard a thing about the getaway car. I went to court to face a couple of misdemeanors . . . breach of peace, obstruction of justice, and some empty beer bottles, and of course I was under age. In return I was kicked off campus but not out of school. Nonetheless, that marked the beginning of my end at Virginia State University.

But first I moved off campus, with a collective of VSU sophomores that I had gotten cool with. One in particular was Ricky, a cool, fly dude from Newport News, and two or three others from New York. There was an irony that I overlooked; back in CT there was a lot of friction between us and the guys from New York. But in VA, because of my accent, and my demeanor, those from the South thought I was from

New York. This made sense but regionally, although there was a lot of overlap, the differences are distinct and nuanced.

While living off campus, still hustling weed, my new roommates are into some other shit, which led to our apartment getting raided. I was asleep on the couch downstairs in the townhouse when the police kicked down the door.

They came in and rounded everybody up, and found everything, including my duffel bag full of weed. Everybody claimed what was theirs, I claimed what was mine. At this point the writing on the wall was clear: *It's time to hit reset*. After several court appearances I received a fine and probation for the weed. I packed up and returned back to Connecticut *bruised, battered, and scarred but hard*. Unaware that those experiences were what was needed for my next encounter with another former Jim Crow South gem awaiting my arrival.

CHAPTER SEVEN
Public Enemy #1: The Superpredators Become Prey

In November of 1993, with both Waterbury and Virginia State behind me, I flew to Atlanta to turn the page on life. At Hartsfield Airport, I called my homie Dread who had moved from Waterbury to Atlanta a few years prior. Dread introduced me to Atlanta and all of its artistry and adventures. He also connected me with some Waterbury legends who I had not known and some who I had only heard about.

When I called Dread he was at the home of a well-known R&B singer/songwriter in Atlanta. Dread, just a few years older than me was plugged-in in Atlanta. Atlanta became fertile ground with the launch of LaFace records. And sensing what was brewing in Atlanta we began strategizing about telling our own stories of growing up and life in CT and all the wild shit we managed to escape. Much of these tells were testimonies that offered hope and a voice to others experiencing the same struggles.

My visit to Atlanta in November 1993 lasted for two weeks and consisted of exploring the well-documented Atlanta night life. I was a 'hood rich 20-year-old from the streets and pretty much down for whatever. The following month, December 1993, I relocated to Atlanta.

The ATL club scene is legendary, and I got there at a time when the city was transitioning. Atlanta was still recovering from the infamous Atlanta child murders, and had just secured the 1996 Olympic bid and was building itself up to be an international attraction. Still in its infancy stage as a burgeoning music Mecca, there were no hip hop radio stations, except for Georgia State College radio on occasion. Old school R&B and Gospel ruled the airwaves, which was a reminder that I was indeed in the South. However, the ideas I had of down south formed from my rural North Carolina experiences as a child, Atlanta helped to gradually eliminate.

With a palm-sized camcorder, I filmed Atlanta in all its '90s glory, like a tourist. I filmed all the marquee and famous spots in Atlanta during my rides around town. I rented a roomy two-bedroom apartment in Northeast Atlanta—I laid it out with a giant, big-screen TV, and all new furniture. I was living good for a 20-year-old man-child who had just hustled his way out of college. With an extended family of people from Waterbury, ranging from a couple years older than me and those from my mother's generation. There was plenty to do in ATL. Magic City and Nikki's back then was like nothing I had ever witnessed, and nothing I had even heard of at the time.

One of the older homies from Waterbury, J. Wes, was the doppelgänger to Chuck D from Public Enemy. Wes was from the Long Hill Projects (LHP), and was the age of my oldest cousins back home, Bo and C-Dale. At that time, Wes had been in ATL for about a decade. Wes carried himself with so much confidence that everywhere we went people were certain that he was someone famous and tried to place him. And in most cases I am sure they thought he was Chuck D. In any case, Wes' presence made everything—and everyone—accessible. The irony was that I eventually met Chuck D years later and worked with him while in Atlanta.

ATL nightlife was immediate and intense, but it faded quickly for me. I had my eye toward a brighter future. And I was actively strategizing to get there—go back to school, entertainment, or both. I came from a family and a community of hustlers who made things happen; like my Cousin Tra Mack but also like my Aunt Maxine and Uncle Bruce who owned businesses and had several income streams in Connecticut.

I asked myself hard questions every day like: *What am I supposed to be doing? Why did I come down here?* Almost immediately, I enrolled in DeKalb Community College, which was a step toward enrolling in Morehouse College, one of my motivations to move to Atlanta.

ATL became a village for folks from Waterbury of various generations. When I got there I was the youngest of everyone who had moved down on their own. We'd have cookouts, hang out, and interact periodically. I was 20 and still growing up in a new hometown.

A friend from back home who I had only vaguely known, we called her "Applebum" (inspired by the song "Bonita Applebum" by A Tribe Called Quest), was part of my regular crew in Atlanta. She was an older "around the way" fly girl, who all hard rocks loved, and everyone respected. One day, Applebum came to my apartment with her two kids, her son Stevie and daughter Tasha, who was about 7 to 8 years old. I was Uncle Manny to them.

Unanticipated Harlem/Waterbury Connection in Atlanta

Applebum's attention was drawn to a framed collection of pictures I had sitting atop of my big-screen TV. Among the pictures was one of my biological father, in the center, and two baby pictures of me on each side.

She grabbed the center photo and turned to me like she'd seen a ghost. Her eyes popped out of her head, her mouth opened with surprise, and she screamed at me, "Butch is your father!"

I wondered, *What . . . ? How do you know that's my father?* I replied, "Yes, he is. But how do you know him?" I asked. Almost no one in Waterbury knew my father. He was born and raised in Harlem. He only came to visit his mother in Waterbury periodically.

Applebum told me that her mother and Butch's mother, DeeDee, were best friends in Harlem and her brothers and Butch grew up together and were like brothers. Applebum's parents had moved to Waterbury from Harlem in the 1970s. She told me that when she was a small girl my father would put her on his shoulders, walk her to the store, buy her candy, and give her money regularly. She said, "The same relationship you have with Tasha (her daughter), is how your father was with me." I was blown away!

I didn't know anybody from home that could tell me much, if anything about him. He was a mystery. Applebum went on further, telling me that her mom was coming to visit Atlanta in a few weeks. "She is not going to believe this, you look just like Butch," she exclaimed, holding back tears. She called her mom and told her about me. When her mother came to Atlanta, she brought pictures of Butch as a young boy and others of my paternal grandmother, DeeDee, who had died young.

I also talked to Applebum's two older brothers who knew Butch. They gave me careful details and insight into his street life growing up in Harlem. I noticed how everybody was careful about what they said about him. It took me traveling 1,000 miles to Atlanta to uncover mysteries from home about my father. It was a revealing period for me in many ways. I would soon have time—too much time—to reflect on it all.

One rainy day, I was driving from Applebum's apartment in Doraville on 85 South. While exiting the highway the wet roads caused me to hydroplane into the opposite lane into oncoming traffic, which caused a head-on collision. Whether from the shock or the crash, I blacked out. I can't recall much after the impact.

The last thing I remembered was exiting the highway and then sitting in the backseat of a DeKalb County police car. What happened immediately after the accident, of which I have some sporadic flashes, was a fistfight between me and others involved in the crash. The police also found a small blunt roach in my ashtray.

I was arrested on four misdemeanor charges—possession of marijuana, driving too fast for conditions, reckless driving, and simple assault. I also totaled my Honda Accord hatchback. I was released immediately after posting a $300 bail. Aside from totaling my car, no big deal. Right?

However, it was 1994. I had just turned 21 and life was already full of action and drama, and unknowingly it was only getting started. I'm not thinking much of the incident but for the back-and-forth court date annoyances. I returned to the community college trying to stay on track with my education.

At this time I was working at Run-and-Shoot Athletic Center on the South-West Side of Atlanta, a popular gym and YMCA-like facility where access and interaction with Black celebrities was common. Run-and-Shoot attracted a who's who of Black celebrities, hoopers and hoop lovers from across the US. I met famous musicians, producers, actors, and those coming up.

In Response to Cee-Lo Green: I Knew Very Little 'bout the Dirty South

Prior to one of my court dates, I got a call from my public defender. Coupled with being naïve and 1,000 miles from home, I underestimated the "justice" system. I decided not to invest in an attorney for misdemeanor charges, thinking a fine and probation was the maximum possible sentence. I was working and going to school full-time and finding my way. Atlanta was treating me well until the call from the public defender, who had asked me to meet him and the district attorney to discuss my case. They recommended that I plead guilty and the "court" was considering upgrading one of the charges from a simple to aggravated assault.

I didn't know what that meant at the time, but I knew it was ridiculous. However, this was 1994: the year that the Crime Bill was signed

112

into law. The Crime bill was written by then Senator Joe Biden and signed into law by President Bill Clinton. Young Black men had become America's scapegoat, were openly hunted, and labeled *super predators*. Official US policy declared (without necessarily naming it as a war on young Black men) that three strikes and you're out. The occupation of Black neighborhoods intensified, police were granted full immunity, licensed to kill and hunt Black men and boys, and in many cases entrap and set us up. Although rates of incarceration started increasing steadily during the mid-1970s, 1994 was pivotal. During the 10 years between 1994 and 2004, incarcerated Americans increased by roughly 1 million from an already staggering record number of around 1.5 to 2.5 million people. Those incarcerated were overwhelmingly Black and Brown men and directly tied to the leverage that the Crime Bill gave local police forces across the US.

I was blind to all of this, but the upgraded aggravated assault charge was the same charge given to someone who shoots a person. According to Georgia law at that time, if you pull out a gun and shoot somebody, and don't kill them, that's aggravated assault. I was overcharged, railroaded, and subsequently wrongfully sent to prison for aggravated assault. I was in prison with many guys serving time for aggravated assault. Many of whom were serving the minimum 10-year suspended after 5-year sentence. In fact, I received the same 10-year sentence suspended after 5 for a fistfight—a legal textbook case of simple assault and a misdemeanor.

My case was heard in DeKalb County, Georgia during the most brutal era of incarceration in US history, post-enslavement. I sat in a courtroom with a formidable Black woman judge—who reminded me of one of my aunts or my mom. Vibrant and seemingly young for a judge. However, the comparisons stopped there. I saw white kids in that courtroom get off the hook with just a scolding here, a few tough words there. However, there was a different standard for Black men. We were sent to lockup and at the age of 22, the year I should have been graduating college, I was about to start the darkest phase of my young life. A 10-year suspended after 5-year sentence in the Georgia Department of Corrections (GA DOC).

I was unexpectedly taken from court and sent to the DeKalb County Jail. A brand new, menacing, high-tech security dungeon, surrounded by unyielding metal and brick. A huge state-of-the-art facility whose timely construction and opening coincided with the passing of the Crime Bill. I had just turned 22 years old, far from home, and caught up in a complex web of national politics reflecting an unaltered violently racist past. Prison ruined my plans. Morehouse seemed out of the question. I did not think that my life was over, but I knew I would be off the streets for a while.

Right after I was arrested, my family begged me to come home. And I thought about it. But, I wasn't trying to be on the run for four misdemeanor charges. Family members from Waterbury were dispatched; my Cousins Tra Mack and his older brother Claudel (C-Dale) drove to Atlanta to lay eyes on me. There was tension between some of my family members and some from the Waterbury village living in Atlanta. My family felt like they should've been looking after me more. But it wasn't that they were not looking after me, because they were. But my family were protective and plus I was my mother's only child. And when my mom, and even more so my grandmother send dispatchers, there were no questions to be asked. Even still, and everyone knew, I was going to do what I wanted.

Before I got sentenced, I was depressed, and my mom was worried. Applebum found a Black psychiatrist in Atlanta who evaluated me and told me to stop smoking weed. Paraphrasing through my vague recollection and lack of knowledge of the field and language of psychiatry, the psychiatrist made some connection to depression and my deep thinking about injustice, along with the stress and trauma of Black life.

During these times, I felt overwhelmed with sadness. And with my family so far away, Applebum was there to remind me: "There's nothing wrong with you." She believed in me more than I believed in myself and pointed out that I was going through a rough patch of my life that I would get through. Even though I could not see how, I chose to believe it. Today, when I talk to Applebum she reminds me of what I overcame and how proud she is of me. However, during this phase of depression many people from Waterbury in Atlanta stayed away from me and wrote me off as having *lost it*. But Applebum had insight, foresight, and integrity. Her love and loyalty amplified when I was at my lowest.

As I reflect on those days, I was angry, hurt, and stressed. I had lost so many friends and loved ones at a young age. Crack cocaine had shifted the paradigm in our communities and transformed what it meant to be Black. New values and ambitions emerged reflective of the worst of capitalism. In my lifetime, the mantra of one of the most iconic Black leaders' and activists' statement, *by any means necessary,* changed. Once the mantra for freedom, justice, and equality, *by any means necessary* for too many of us came to mean, *get money.* Get money *by any means necessary.* And it did not matter whose family you had to traumatize.

I was stressed and depressed about my naïve involvement in all of the culture shifting dynamics happening in Waterbury and in Black communities throughout the US. I had not realized that running away from my recent past to Atlanta's beautiful women, parties, and camcorder-captured *fun* could not treat my trauma.

GA DOC: Grieving and Healing in all the Wrong Places

I found my young mind in a deep state of reflection regarding the deaths of Ragar Overstreet and Chris Love. Amplified by the death of my father and reflections from people who knew him. Although some time had passed since my mother told me about his death, I never processed it. I had stored it away and never mentioned it again until I was 20, right before I moved to Atlanta. I had no idea that I was grieving. Or even what it meant to grieve at that time.

In the backdrop of all of this, five of the most valuable years of my life had been remanded to the Georgia Department of Corrections. After several months in the DeKalb County Jail I was transferred to Jackson State Penitentiary for diagnostic testing and classification. Jackson held Georgia's death row inmates as they awaited being put to death. One of Georgia's most infamous death row inmates, Wayne Williams, was there when I got there. Wayne Williams was the face of the infamous Atlanta child murders. I remembered as a child in Waterbury hearing about the mysterious murders of young Black kids throughout Atlanta. I did not grow up in Atlanta, but I have personally never met anyone from Atlanta who believed Williams killed the 29 mostly Black male children ages 15 and younger from ATLs poorest most divested communities. I met individuals from those communities and neighborhoods who, as children, lived through the fears of coming up dead and who were relatives and friends of those who were mysteriously killed.

Nonetheless, here I was, held against my will—the *property* of the State of Georgia—in the literal shadow of death for several months. Surveilled and closely monitored while undergoing IQ and personality tests. I was lauded by counselors due to my 115 IQ score, which according to their standards was above average. My IQ score became a theme with each new prison counselor and facility that I entered in the Georgia Department of Corrections. I remember being unfazed by their evaluation and assessment of me. Because even then I knew that their standards and methods were bullshit.

After Jackson, I was assigned to a county camp: Hall County, in Gainesville, Georgia. Inmates at Jackson who were deemed *non-violent, low flight risks* were *rewarded* with better food, workout equipment, and local daytime jobs in a county camp. However, the county camps in Georgia were essentially *modern* slave encampments under the guise of more freedom of movement. At county camps, like Hall, inmates worked throughout Hall

County and did many of the city and county's jobs for zero pay. I, and fellow prisoners worked the recycling plants, drove asphalt trucks, shoveled asphalt, filled potholes, paved streets and roads. Inmates worked and maintained the city and county's fleet of government vehicles. Park and recreation detail as in cleaning the parks, cutting and trimming trees. Trash pick-up in the streets and on highways. Hall County held 250 inmates and those of us who had a skill or the capacity to learn one had it exploited. Otherwise you wound up doing any of the multitude of unskilled jobs like picking up trash or working in the recycling plant. And if you bucked against any of that you were sent to one of the 23-hour state lockdown facilities.

The metaphorically *modernized* plantation and slave tactics in the county camps in Georgia made tangible the dehumanizing experiences of my ancestors before *escaping* the tobacco fields in NC.

After nearly 3 years in Hall County, I was transferred to a halfway house in midtown Atlanta—the Atlanta Transition Center (ATC). I had 2 years left on my 5-year sentence. During the Crime Bill, tough on crime-era parole was hard to come by; almost everyone was maxing out their sentence.

I met some of the most brilliant Black men while incarcerated in GA. Many memorable for their intelligence, and an array of various other traits and talents. Like Kenny Phelps. His father was a well-known scientist whose work and research had been highlighted on the Discovery Channel. However, his son, Kenny, was serving a life sentence. Kenny had a college degree from a prestigious East Coast university and his intellectual labor was put to use in Georgia's Governor's mansion as an inmate in the ATC. Kenny also wrote the curriculum for the GED program at the ATC, and was often called upon for an array of administrative work at the ATC. I spent much of my time in the ATC picking Kenny's brilliant brain.

While at the ATC I worked at one of the State agencies in downtown ATL on MLK Jr. Drive. I was on a three-man detail that maintained and monitored the fleet of State vehicles. Many of the State's shot callers were housed in that building, and most important among them, for us at least, were the members of Georgia's Board of Pardon and Parole. I learned their faces and their record on parole. There were three of them: a Black woman, a Black man, and white man and we would see and interact with them briefly and sporadically. I would strike up small talk with them whenever they came through in their black State-issued Ford Crown Victoria's.

One day, I initiated a conversation with the Black woman parole board member telling her my story behind the crime in which I was convicted. As I explained my case, I remember her sitting back in her seat unable to hide her shock. Knowing that she could easily pull my file and call my bluff if I were lying, I gave her as many details and nuances as I could fit into my 45-second pitch that I had practiced at this point for almost four years. A few days later, I had the exact same conversation with the Black male parole board member. After having these talks and seeing the reactions they conjured, it felt possible that I would get some consideration.

I did not know what was going to happen but I felt a sense of relief as though I had been heard, finally, by someone who could do something.

Within a week, I was paged and summoned to the Corrections Officer station in the ATC. I needed a local Atlanta address because I was unexpectedly granted parole. That was the best feeling I had felt over the past 49 months. Perhaps this was the feeling my ancestors felt driving from pitch-black Tarboro Road in NC when they reached the bright lights of NYC. I was 26 years old and had to get my feet underneath me and back to my life, nearly blind to the next chapters.

CHAPTER EIGHT

Atlanta and Hip Hop Culture: The Calm Before the Takeover

To be clear, being locked up in Georgia was daunting. But Black history is filled with resilience and overcoming. And examples of making miracles from oppression and struggle. So there were some silver-linings worth mentioning during my years locked up. I was already a reader; while locked up I became an avid reader. I also started writing rhymes and telling my life stories. I was locked up with individuals from some of the most thorough Atlanta neighborhoods. Many became friends. We exchanged stories, mutual admiration and respect. I was incarcerated with guys who were related to many of the rappers, went to school, or grew up with them. And as ATL's hip hop scene began to surge, it was dope to watch them watch their childhood friends and relatives climb out of the mud and become local, national, and even international celebrities and heroes.

Hip hop was attractive to me because it was one of the few spaces in America where you were not required to seek approval or surrender to the ways of white people. We could express ourselves freely, and construct counternarratives about Black life and the environments that we inherited. Hip hop was a much better alternative than the fakery asked of us in schools. Hip hop culture unsuspectedly represented the biggest counter to common American myths and tropes. Rap artists exposed the depths of American hypocrisy and corruption by simply telling their stories of survival. The descendants of the survivors of the Middle Passage, Enslavement, and Jim Crow built a platform from scraps found in the pits of America's ghettos. Poetic renditions of navigating divested communities, systemically under-resourced and failed schools, and unimaginable forms of impoverishment carved out a new international following. A new market-economy emerged from nothing and became an American cultural juggernaut and cash cow, which inevitably was overrun by corporate, capitalist vultures.

But hip hop became a legitimate hustle and an escape from poverty and the risks associated with the streets. However, that changed at the height of its popularity with the violent murders of hip hop royalty such as Tupac, Biggie, and later Nipsey Hussle and Atlanta legend Takeoff from the group Migos.

Moving to Atlanta in 1993 allowed me to witness the birth of a new rendition and expansion of hip hop. Atlanta's stronghold and influence in hip hop and pop culture today resembles NYC in the 1980s and 1990s. Ironically, I sat front row for both the East Coast explosion and Atlanta's takeover. But in 1993 I do not believe anyone could have predicted Atlanta's place in hip hop lore today. I think many understood the potential, which is why ATL became a Mecca of sorts and a refuge for so many pro-Black Blackamericans across the nation. Yet in 1993, although bubbling beneath the surface, Atlanta was still untapped. The access to young Black celebrities at the time is unheard of today. I recall one of many memorable stories at a local spot, Club Diamonds. Diamonds was near my apartment and we were regulars, went there to eat, listen to music, and shoot pool. We knew some of the ladies who worked there and some of my older homies knew some individuals who worked in management. One random weeknight we walked into Diamonds and the first person I see inside was Tupac Shakur. This particular night Diamonds was not crowded, but Tupac stood patiently at the picture booth, with a line of women waiting to take pictures with him. This was shortly after Pac had shot two off-duty Atlanta cops who were drunk and harassing folks in downtown. This was after the release of the movie *Juice*, but before *Death Row*, and before the international megastar he eventually became.

I remember making eye contact with Pac and we shared the traditional head nod of respect and acknowledgement that Black men do, but we never spoke. I have no claim to Pac. But I regret not approaching him. Just to look him in the eye and shake his hand, maybe take a picture with him. But that version of myself thought I would have come across like a groupie and my friends would have had jokes for years. Although I had no claim to fame, I was a young hustler with jewelry and money; I thought I was the shit, too. Just by watching his moves from a distance, I recall how energetic he was. His vibrations were powerful even though he hardly moved from the one spot he was in while we were there. I could feel how real, grounded, and down to earth he was. We were both kids. Pac was two years older—I was 20 and he was 22. Three years later, while I was in Hall

County locked down, Pac was murdered. Another powerful Black life taken too soon. Like Sonnet, the kid from VSU; just a head nod and a silent salute.

Back to the Essence

The photos in my head of that era are vivid, and music played a big role. The music helped me reflect and process all that I was going through. The various stages of turmoil later contributed to the inspiration for my own musical content and entrepreneurial aspirations.

And although I sat front row to witness Atlanta's hip hop takeover, I also had a unique bird's eye view of hip hop's premature years in New York City, before it travelled the country and became an international phenomenon. There is very little documentation about hip hop's first audiences outside of NYC. However, Connecticut, undoubtedly, was one of the genres earliest soundboards and a critical litmus test for early hip hop pioneers. Connecticut is geographically north of New York City, a 30-minute to 2-hour drive, depending on where you are coming from in NYC and where you are going in Southern Connecticut. And there is much overlap between Southern Connecticut and NYC. Southern Connecticut comprises bedroom towns and suburbs of NYC. Many people live in Southern Connecticut and work in NYC. And many New Yorkers preferred Southern Connecticut for smaller, less crowded cities and towns to raise families. And long before satellite radio, internet, and the various seamless ways that music travels today, in hip hop's infancy, if you were not on the East Coast, the Northeast specifically, you were left behind musically. But Southern Connecticut was within the radio frequency of New York City radio.

In other words, as the music was being produced and created in NYC and broadcasted on local radio stations, Southern Connecticut, Northern New Jersey, and the five boroughs in New York City were the first audience and consumers of the new artists and their music. There were two pioneering and trailblazing radio stations at the time in NYC: 98.7 Kiss FM and 107.5 WBLS. Both traversed the airwaves throughout Southern Connecticut. We listened to and audio-recorded the hip hop shows and became familiar with the radio personalities Mr. Magic and Marley Marl, Red Alert and Chuck Chill Out. In Waterbury we were well-versed in hip hop's evolution, the new and ground-breaking songs and artists. We went to school or hung out in our neighborhoods and talked enthusiastically and scholarly about music that was enlightening us and shaping our minds. I was able to record, what became iconic moments and *world premieres* in hip hop. For example, I was tape-recording the night that Mr. Magic premiered the song "Public Enemy #1" by Public Enemy (PE) on his Rap Attack show on 107.5 WBLS. Magic is infamous for wrongly declaring PE was lyrically weak and that they would not last long in hip hop. I'm part of that first generation of Connecticut scribes of hip hop. We are part of the genesis: grios, students, and hip hop historians.

Hip Hop's East Coast Bias

While growing up many of my friends and peers in the Northeast/East Coast rejected much of the music that wasn't from our region. However, unlike many of my friends and peers, I grew up listening to NWA, Compton's Most Wanted, Spice 1, Cam, Ice Cube, Lynch Mob, UGK and Scarface as enthusiastically as I did the Jungle Brothers, BDP, X-Clan, Poor Righteous Teachers, Gangstarr, Public Enemy, A Tribe Called Quest, and De La Soul. Friends often hated riding in my car because of the high probability that I might be playing some West Coast or Southern artists who they had never heard of. I listened to everything, studiously. Amid the different accents and word choices I could hear the same struggles and goals of my peers from across the country in places where I had never heard of. That open mind-state helped me when I got to Atlanta.

November 19, 1993 the Outkast song and video "Players Ball" was released. About three weeks after the murder of C-Love and one week before my first ever visit to Atlanta. In recalling their lyrics "all the players came from far and wide, wearing afros and braids . . . now I'm here to tell you, there's a better day . . . ." Outkast was so fresh, raw, and different and almost resoundingly rejected by my friends and peers back home at first. But even more, Outkast was summoning me to ATL. And in a way, they summoned the like-minded pro-Black among us to Atlanta in hopes of "a better day." In any case, I was rocking with Outkast. Although I never got the chance to meet them while living in Atlanta, we shared several mutual acquaintances and I would see them around town.

126

James "Manny" Wright

By the time I got out of prison in 1999, Atlanta's hip hop scene had unstoppable momentum and Outkast were superstars leading the charge.

My friend Swain from VSU, who moved to ATL right after I did, had held onto all of my possessions while I was locked up. During my four years in prison, Swain was finishing up his degree in film production at Clark Atlanta University.

That same year I met filmmaker, producer, and writer, Gia'na Garel. Gia'na, having seen my interest in the music industry, supported my efforts to build a label. After she heard some of my music and the artists I was shopping as part of a production deal, she called me and said "Hey, I want to take you to meet Chuck." I thought, there is only one *Chuck* she could be talking about. But I asked anyway, "Chuck who?" The Chuck D of Public Enemy. Gia'na had a working relationship and a direct line to Chuck. She had shared with him my vision and what I had been working on musically, and he agreed to meet me.

It is impossible to exaggerate the impact that Chuck and PE had on enlightening me on Black history and culture growing up. Musically, PE was at the forefront of providing a Black curriculum that encouraged me to read more about Black leaders, struggles, and resistance across the diaspora. They put *music in their message* and told the world, without any mediators or filters, about what was happening to the historically disenfranchised Blacks in the US.

127

I met Chuck somewhere in South Atlanta at his home. I played some of the music that I had. I had a collective of folks from Waterbury, Atlanta, and Charlotte. I had built a relationships with a dope music producer from Charlotte named WIZdom. WIZ was an inhouse producer for Soulife Records, which contributed to the neo-soul movement of the 2000s. But WIZ had hip hop aspirations as well and his own crew of MCs from the Carolinas including his younger brother, Mel. I met them through their cousin who was living in Atlanta. WIZ, Mel, and I bonded instantly and they became my brothers. I loved WIZ and Mel musically and for who they were as individuals. They were born and raised in South Carolina; they were part of the home-base who stayed behind as many of our ancestors fled Jim Crow during the Great Migration. And like I said, our survival, as Blackamericans, hinged on both branches: those who left and those who stayed. Wiz and Mel loved, supported and championed what I was doing musically and I felt the same way about them. We were each other's cheerleaders and motivation.

The one song that stood out most to Chuck was a song that I rapped over on a beat from WIZ and a verse from Mel. Chuck asked to put that song on his internet indie label *SlamJamz*. Free, international publicity from my childhood hero and a living legend? It was a no brainer. I also started my own label Thoroughbred Entertainment and Chuck volunteered to do the artwork and graphic designs. I had music mogul ambitions, I envisioned myself scouting talent and putting the right pieces together. I had a great ear for music and I was in the South admiring Master P and Cash Money Records and calculating how to craft my own lane based off of elements of their blueprint featuring artists from Connecticut and my other connections I had established while in Atlanta.

Through some connections that I had made through Chuck and Gia'na, I ended up in California. By this time, Swain had graduated from Clark Atlanta and was working and politicking his film production aspirations in Cali. I would eventually connect with him for the short time I was there.

While in Cali I started having revelations and reservations about the music industry. Some of the people and artists that I wanted to represent, especially the ones in Waterbury, were not as serious or motivated as I thought they needed to be. But more importantly, I began reflecting on what got me through the four years of lockdown. Islam grounded me and taught me patience, and helped me regain and maintain my sanity. It helped me to grow spiritually, mentally, and emotionally in the most unremarkable of physical places. As a result I began to struggle with the music industry doors that were opening up and all of the elements that came with that. And I was also being pulled back into the same streets and practices that I had run away from almost 10 years ago. I had to decide whether to continue that path or pursue a spiritual journey and quest I was being called toward. I had made a few handshake agreements to promote music from talented individuals who entrusted me with their musical aspirations. And I had visions of helping some of the most talented artists find a lane. I was confident that I could have helped launch some new stars and place Waterbury on the map. And I was willing to do the leg work to help my friends get in the music industry.

Change of Heart

Ultimately I came to terms that a career in the music industry, whether successful or not, would not have satisfied me. I was not content with living the life chasing a career in the music industry. I had become content reading and learning about creation and the Creator and issues around life and death. Examining the purpose of life gave me comfort and solace. And this was what I wanted to explore. The scholar in me poured into more books and deep knowledge that put me at ease with a lot of the turmoil that was happening in my life. This path mitigated the anger and stress in me and placed me on a journey of understanding. The genetic coils of tension and rage bound up in me were loosened. I was reminded how that relief helped me get through the hardest thing that I ever had to deal with.

I dropped everything and left Cali and returned to Connecticut. I needed to strategize and figure out my next move. I stayed in Connecticut and did that. I went to the mosque every day. And although I was not guaranteed anything, I feel like my entrance into the music industry was likely had I stayed the course. But I felt relief and I wanted to explore more of what helped me to, not only manage, but maintain and even grow while locked up 1,000 miles away from home in a Georgia chain gang. I was determined to learn how to read Arabic and the Quran and the Islamic sciences.

I spoke to some Muslim elders back in Connecticut about places that I could go. Egypt was a suggestion, as many young men and women from throughout the US had gone and studied in Cairo.

I learned about several schools and institutes designed to teach Arabic to foreigners. One of the elders, a university professor and a mentor, along with one of the local imams consoled me regarding my aspirations and they had Egyptian connections. My life was about to take a turn that I did not see coming. I hadn't expected at any stage of my life to find my story being written out in desert lands in Arabic.

CHAPTER NINE
الجذور—Replanted Roots

On my trip to Cairo, I felt home on arrival . . .
Nas is good
— Nas

Egypt. I knew the moment that the plane landed that I was in place far different than anyplace I had ever been. And like so many of my other life adventures I did not know what to expect and could not imagine what was awaiting me. Nonetheless, it felt oddly familiar; perhaps due to the signs and clues that led me there. Egypt is in Africa—the land of my fore-forefathers, and the land where my spirit and consciousness reached a level of elevation difficult to articulate.

Writing about how I got there is easy. But reflecting on the hardships that led to a level of consciousness to consider going and then pulling it off, was cathartic. I had researched and cross-referenced with friends and mentors about a place to study before leaving. I decided on a well-known institute in Cairo. I contacted the school's administrators, who coordinated with me online regarding course options, housing, and airport pickup.

132

I landed in Cairo around noon in the middle of the brutal August heat in 2003. I was overdressed; designer Sean John jeans, Timberland boots, and a long-sleeve cotton button-down shirt. The sun felt as though you could reach out and touch it.

I waited in the airport terminal for the representatives from the Arabic Language Center to pick me up. Two young men held up signs with my and the center's name on it. I greeted them, and we exited. By the time we reached the car, I was covered in so much sweat that I could wring the bottom of my shirt. Once in the car, they handed me a water bottle and we drove off. The institute was approximately a 30-minute drive from the airport to Medina Nasr or Nasr City, a populous, cosmopolitan section of Cairo. I was eager but exhausted from travelling and quickly became disappointed because my living arrangements were unsettled, although I was told they were before I left the US. Once at the center, they assured me that they were still working it out.

I sat in the waiting area of the institute while the two center administrators appeared to be busy working on my housing arrangements. While waiting, tired, sweaty, and hot, a tall, bright-faced young man bops from the back area from his class. He spoke to me in a distinct British accent and assumed rightfully that I was from the US. We talked briefly, and he asked where I was staying. I told him that I was waiting for the two employees to verify a place. His name was Shuaib, and he immediately advised, "Don't take a flat from them; they are going to overcharge you."

After a 12-hour direct flight from JFK in New York City to Cairo, that was the last thing I wanted to hear. I was at a crossroads between my old life (which had become as hot as the sun above me, and I needed to cool off) and my new life, as wide open as the Egyptian sands. But at this point, I just wanted to get into a place, freshen up, and relax.

"Do you know anyone here?" Shuaib asked. I was still in a chaotic limbo, so I shrugged, "I just landed and came straight here from the airport. I know a couple of people here, but I haven't contacted anyone yet," I explained.

Shuaib suggested his apartment. He said that "I have a place within walking distance from here. I've got three roommates. We're all students here." He explained that one of his roommates was heading back to the UK in a few days, and I could take his room if I wanted. When he told me the price I almost accepted the offer without even looking. His offer was substantially cheaper that what I was quoted online. "If you want, when I'm done with my class, I can walk you over there, it's right around the corner, and you can see it for yourself and decide," he offered.

Having been raised by the streets, I have a strong sense of when I am being played and when someone is being straight up with me. It was easy to see that Shuaib was sincere and for whatever reason wanted to look out for me. A few minutes later he returned and said, "you can leave your stuff here for now, and we'll come right back," he told me. We left the institute and walked 10 minutes away to see the flat, which was sufficient and in a nice area of Nasr City called Haya Thaman, or area 8.

I thought about his offer and the price. I could trust either the institute to settle housing arrangements (and so far they hadn't) or this 21-year-old kid that rolled up on me out of nowhere. Shuaib, although young, was a mature, cheerful, and loving old soul. I sensed it right away, and as I got to know him, I saw how everyone he encountered gravitated and adored him. It was amazing that this would be my very first interaction not even an hour into my journey into Egypt. A clear God-send was placed in my path to help guide my steps (and spare my pockets). In any event, I agreed to take the room he offered. I got to know the other roommates as well, one of whom was from the Midwest in the US. I was searching to heal from all that I put myself through from my past in Waterbury, VSU, and Atlanta. Egypt felt promising. Opened doors and some incredible new friends were on the horizon.

Later that day, Shuaib took me shopping, and soon after we returned, I was ready to settle in for my first night's sleep in a strange but promising new land. I laid in bed and replayed the last 10 years of my life in my head. I was overwhelmed reflecting on all that it took for me to get here. Even further, reflecting on my roots and origins, at least those that were not detached and cut off from me. My post-enslavement lineage was all I knew. The transatlantic human trafficking racket and its cartels destroyed more than can ever be repaired or replaced. Reflecting on myself in context of my family tree, I, like those before me, had to navigate racialized systems and landmines in order to grow. Growing up surrounded by untimely deaths, inexplicable oppression, injustice, and inherited ancestral trauma had taken a toll on me. I arrived in Egypt 30 years young and at a crossroad—a stranger more defiant path than anyone expected. I shut off my brain and went to sleep.

A Call to Something Greater than Myself

The following morning, I woke up to the call-to-prayer (the Athan)—blaring across the city. The windows in my room were opened, which amplified the seemingly omnipresent boom signaling the urgency and significance of the call.

Pulled from bed by loudspeakers from across the city, I was unprepared for this breathtaking experience. Although a relatively new Muslim, this was not my first encounter with hearing the Athan. However, hearing it in a Muslim country was surreal, and I was blown away by the power of its appeal. I was overcome with an indescribable feeling of relief from past fears and the certainty that I was "home." Not home in the sense that Egypt was my home but as a part of Africa, the continent itself. Perhaps these ancient feelings were transmitted through my DNA, and after centuries away, my connection to my family's genetic memory still carried the familiarity of the land? I don't know; maybe that's a reach. But that first night and morning in Egypt was one of the most surreal feelings I had ever had up to that point in my life. It helped lead to a new awareness, a third path at the crossroads—not left nor right—but straight.

All these years later I still do not have the right words; those feelings do not have a name, and they are not a part of any academic discourse that I know of. Whenever friends back in the US would ask me about my experiences in Egypt, I recall that first night and morning in the city. In hindsight, I was being signaled that my life was about to change forever. Eager and open to connect with the continent and all the possibilities stirred strong emotions and an overflow of tears.

In Cairo I met other Americans from across the US, mainly from the Northeast Corridor and the Midwest. Many of us remain close friends to this day, Blackamerican ex-pats and Muslim reverts. I also made acquaintances with many others from Canada, and many other Western nations, UK, France, and across Western Europe. They were like-minded young Westerners who had left modern societies looking for a life of peace in so-called third world Egypt. Entrepreneurs, teachers, professionals, lawyers, doctors, and even ex-convicts trying to change their lives and form bonds.

We didn't know each other, but we were brought to a single place to get closer to Allah, and as a result, many of us became brothers. It was a brotherhood that I never had experienced before and needed.

Brand Nubians: One for All

Of all the introductions and new opportunities that opened up in Egypt, marriage and the birth of my three sons were the most life-changing. I met Layla through mutual friends. I wasted little time meeting with her family and stating my intentions to marry her.

I wanted to explore all the aspects of growing into the man I wanted to become—a serious student of knowledge, a husband, and a father.

Layla was a stunningly beautiful dark-brown woman with an infectious personality and soothing voice. Layla was from a distinguished Nubian tribe, Abu Simbel, and meeting her family was intimidating. Many of Layla's prominent and dignified family members consisted of educators, including professors, teachers and administrators, entrepreneurs, politicians, government officials, and military war heroes.

Her father was a former United Nations employee in Cairo who passed away before she and I met. His photos resembled familiar distinguished Black men, dark radiant brown skin, and deep brown eyes. Her mother was the most regal Black woman I had ever seen. The moment I saw her mother, I was captivated. It was like starring at a glaringly bright light; in her early '60s at the time, she beamed of grace and regality and was among the most humble persons I had ever known.

When my mom came to visit us in Cairo soon after our marriage, Layla's mom prepared every meal as if she was feeding a dignitary. My mom was in awe of Layla's family's hospitality.

She always talked about Layla's mom's insistence on removing the bones from my mom's fish before eating. And many other red carpet treatments, such as elaborate, multicourse meals, every day of her stay.

I often reflect back to Ms. Norman, my Wilby High School teacher, telling us about her experiences in Africa and first introducing the word—Nubia—to me earlier in life. This one high school teacher planted a seed and left a light on for the dark journey ahead. I was a high school kid imagining the wonders and beauty of the ancient Nubians, who left behind world marvels and civilizational wonders that stretched back thousands of years. The implications of Nubian history and dispelling Eurocentric myths about the Black diaspora are profound, and they stayed with me.

When I first thought of going to Egypt it had not crossed my mind that I was going to a place inhabited, still, by Nubians and that had no impact on my decisions at all.

It only hit my radar once I got there. Now, engaging with Nubians, who some Blackamericans mythicized, was special, but to become part of their family was beyond my imagination back at Wilby. Meeting Layla and her Nubian family was another thread that fate wove into my Egyptian experience.

As a "Nubian" in her own words, she told me who Nubians were historically and currently. Like many Blackamericans, I thought Nubia and Nubians were metaphors for Black royalty. Until Mrs. Norman's class at Wilby, I had not known that they were ancient people who contributed immensely to ancient civilizations' glory, notably Ancient Egypt. They are unmistakably melanin-rich, but like other Blacks in the diaspora, their pigment and skin tones range from the deepest dark to brown, light, and fair-skinned.

I often passed for Nubian while in Egypt, and if they were in the US, they could easily be mistaken for homegrown Blackamericans.

The Nubian Museum: Black Royalty on Display

A couple of years after we married, we visited Layla's Nubian village—Abu Simbel—in Aswan for Eid. Meeting more of her family members and a trip to the Nubian Museum in Aswan added additional layers of wonder to my Egyptian journey. We stayed with Layla's father's sister, also named Layla. Auntie Layla, as she was affectionately referred to, was small in stature with deep dark beautiful skin and blue eyes.

I reciprocated the adoration that she showed me. One of the things I learned amongst the Nubians and, to some degree, some of the Egyptians in general, is that if they like and admire you, their interactions with you left no doubt. Similarly, if they did not like you, there would be little if any pretense.

I was escorted around Abu Simbel by Layla's uncle, her father's youngest brother, Sha'ban, who was just a few years older than me. Abu Simbel is a section or a branch of Nuba's 40-something tribes, and Nuba's most famous tribe and where the Queen Nefertari descended. the Temple of Abu Simbel is a modern marvel and a UNESCO world heritage site. Historically, Nubians did not mix much with Arabs, Greeks, and other groups who settled in Egypt. Thus, their African essence remains apparent; their resistance to outside marriage posed some difficulties, but Layla's mom was supportive despite some other detractors in her family. The decision to marry was ultimately left up to Layla.

Once married, the birth of three sons soon followed—each born over the next few years in a Cairo hospital overlooking the Nile River. The birth of my three sons added another branch to my family's tree, with roots replanted on the dark continent that brought forth the light of civilization and is the birthplace of humanity. I had come home, but what a rough path of return.

Over the nearly six years I lived in Egypt, seeds were planted that led to deep learning and growth toward the scholarly, grounded man many had envisioned. My study of Arabic and various Islamic sciences became soul food that was integral to my healing.

We built a flat on land that Layla inherited from her deceased father. The result was a three-bedroom flat, not too far from the Corniche, which is a strip of the Nile River. My last two sons were born while living in this particular flat. We partnered with another Nubian family and opened a grocery store in the same Cairo suburb. In reflection, my life and my understanding of life had changed fundamentally—mentally and spiritually. Things were going well due to a collective of supportive in-laws, particularly my mother-in-law; her name and reputation carried much weight.

I've seen foreigners, like me, move abroad and get their money or businesses taken from them or forced into other legal logjams. My in-laws made sure none of that happened to me. Nubians have a stellar reputation throughout Egypt, and the family I married into personified that. When we built our flat, Layla's cousin oversaw and managed the building project, and regarding the store, our Nubian partners identified and negotiated with vendors. There were newfound successes and many great experiences in Egypt after many ups and downs in the US.

However, another aspect of Egypt reminded me of the worst of my Blackamerican experiences back home. I recognized horrifying anti-Blackness in Egypt that was vivid and vocal. It is not systemic and foundational to the country like in the US, but perhaps a remnant of its colonial past. Many societies and peoples investments in whiteness led to their adopting anti-Blackness and anti-Black ideas and practices, even on the dark continent rooted in Blackness. However, the US provided me with the tools to balance a troubling anti-Black aspect in Egypt.

My oldest son attended a reputable private school in Egypt from kindergarten 'til third grade and was an excellent student, and I had high hopes. Upon our return to the states in his fourth-grade year, though, he had his first white teacher, a man, who labeled him and made him question himself and his abilities. This treatment was very typical of US schools. Even though academically my son was supported and thrived in school while in Egypt, there was a problematic undercurrent of anti-Blackness that he experienced that only revealed itself to me years later. Anti-Blackness is prevalent in North Africa and throughout the Muslim world in general and is not talked about enough. Although anti-Blackness preceded colonialism, the *modern* systems and institutions of racism that exist currently are byproducts of European colonialism and have been exacerbated over the past five-centuries. One of the indelible trademarks of white supremacy is evidenced by internalized colonization, historically Black societies seeking to mimic whiteness and Eurocentric norms and values.

142

I have heard some Egyptians, for example, express to me that Egypt is not in Africa. Instead, they argued, it is in the *Middle East* and that the ancient Egyptians weren't Black and the Blacks in Egypt did not contribute to any of the country's past glory and so on. I understand the power of Eurocentric ideology and discourse, and I experienced its impact on ordinary everyday Egyptians. However, this was just one of many points of view and I am not saying it was the dominant one, but it is notable for the sake of the discussion on anti-Blackness, which unfortunately was very pervasive.

Reflecting on my experiences are not meant to sow more discord. My hope is to recognize and begin some serious discussions regarding the residue of colonization—the white supremacy and the anti-Blackness that it exacerbated. These are my good and bad experiences in a country that I not just visited but where I lived, started a family, owned property, and educated my sons and myself. And in many respects rescued me from my experiences in the US and gave me grace for renewal.

Unconventional Study Abroad

While at the Arabic Learning Institute, I agreed to work privately with one of the instructors for additional tutoring. He had a doctorate in the Islamic sciences and is a widely known and notable scholar. I visited his home 5 to 6 days a week over the course of the several years that I lived in Egypt. I built a relationship with him, I ate with him and his family, and they treated me like family. He didn't speak English, and he never tried. For me to

143

effectively communicate with him, I had to meet him on his terms. All of the sciences and books that we read were in the classical Arabic text, and I struggled immensely early on learning Arabic. But he was patient and made it intriguing; I had never in my life been so studious.

My life in Egypt helped me re-analyze and re-set life away from a troubled past. I had immersed myself in a once-in-a-lifetime experience that even deep-rooted racial constructs and divides couldn't prevent or erase.

My Arabic tutor asked me about my degree status back in the US. I told him I had started college, but I didn't finish, leaving out the details about my past life and the old me left back in America. He encouraged, "Go back and get your degree . . . Go back and finish!" I wondered, take the new me back home and immerse myself in education even with all its woven racism and a society I had, for a time, given up on? Had I recovered, healed enough? Was my armor strong enough to return home? Yet family waited whose voices rang out and vibrated to me like the early morning call to prayer.

CHAPTER TEN
Coming Home

While living in Egypt, married, with two sons at the time, a grocery store, a mind for study, and prolific teachers and mentors, my mom informed me of Leonard Williams. Leonard and mom fell in love, married a short time after, and purchased a house in the East End of Waterbury. A few months after moving into their home, Leonard was diagnosed with cancer—multiple myeloma—and rapidly declined. I called home several times a week. Every time I called my mom assured me that everything was ok. During one call, though, several of my mom's sisters were in town from North Carolina as Leonard's condition worsened.

After passing the phone around to my aunts who had been there helping my mom, one of my aunt's said to me, "You realize that you have to come home, right?" Shocked, I gullibly asked why. She explained that Leonard's condition had worsened. My mom found herself in a new house too big for just herself. My aunt gave it to me raw—my mom would need help maintaining all of these new circumstances with the inevitable passing away of her recently wed husband.

I realized that Mom, true to form, had misinformed me and had me believing that everything was alright. Still in Egypt, I had to rethink everything. How will I leave and when? What about the store? Initially, I planned to return to the US for a short stay. But once I returned home I realized the gravity of my mom's situation and felt compelled to stay as long as necessary. I arrived to watch Leonard's last two weeks of life. I was heartbroken for my mom and also Leonard's family, some of whom I had known prior to his marriage to my mom.

After the funeral, I stayed in CT with my mom and since I was there I returned to school. I enrolled in an accelerated bachelor's program at Post University in the West End of Waterbury.

Misinformation Guised as Higher Learning

My most memorable experience at Post reminded how misinformation spun, which makes learning in the US challenging and teaching frustrating. A Post University professor discussing the war in the Sudan referred to the Sudanese people as Arabs.

I was fresh from the region, having known and befriended many Sudanese, and found myself in class led by a clueless white man misinforming us about geopolitics and ethnic Africans. He was clearly making distinctions due to borders contrived by Europeans that separated tribes and kin due to European imaginations and interests. His ignorance was too much to bear and he forced me to speak out after he described the "conflict" as Arabs in the North vs Christian Africans in the South. I was appalled by this, at best, reckless conflation. Having literally just returned from the region after living there for six years, I had come to know Sudanese who were living in Cairo, from both North and South Sudan.

146

Now granted the North and South of Sudan was and is primarily divided by Northern Sudanese who are Muslim and practice Islam and the South many who are Christian. But what is unmistakable to me is that they are—both North and South Sudanese—Africans. They are unmistakably "Black" people, as if the name of the country itself does not attest to that—Bilad As-Sudan—*the land of the Blacks.* Many of the Northern Sudanese that I met and came in contact with while in Cairo, along with the Nubians, reminded me most of the Blacks in the US who I was related to and who I grew up around. So for this professor to suggest that they were Arab was factually wrong.

During his lecture, I corrected him and told him that the Northern Sudanese were not Arab but in fact African. He was shocked, appalled, and, obviously, not used to being challenged or corrected in class. He reiterated his position and I, mine. He added that because they were Muslim and spoke Arabic, they were Arab and felt the need to remind us that the South Sudanese were Christian. I told him both people were African and that although the Northern Sudanese spoke Arabic it didn't make them Arab, no more than my speaking English made me *English.* I had to remind him that one's tongue or language does not determine their identity, ethnicity, or *race.* We went back and forth and some of my classmates were visibly shook due to the tension in the room. I am generally wise about picking my battles and sometimes I let these types of ignorant-based quarrels slide, but I challenged everything he said. I realized that his mind was already set, so my goal was to offer the class an alternative view on the issue and to be better informed.

About ten years later, a girl from my class approached me and recalled that conversation and how stunned she was but proud of my stance. At the time, however, I had no visible allies, and clearly was on my own in the discussion. But I was happy to hear that the push back resonated with someone years later.

Committed to a Long Educational Haul

I dug my heels in and decided to finish my studies in the US while my partners and Layla ran the store back in Egypt. I was juggling life between continents, managing my new family in Egypt and a business, while in the US helping my mom. Mom was far too stubborn to admit or say that it was hard or that she needed help; she's not built that way. I told her, "I'm going to stay for a while." She was happy but concerned, "What about the kids and Layla?"

I told her that I'll keep them in school. We had a stable income from the store and enough to maintain them. I told her I'd stay, get a job, finish school, visit when I can, and bring them to the US in the summers. I finished my bachelor's at Post University in two years while working full-time. I graduated with honors with a bachelor's in business administration. I then enrolled in Southern Connecticut State University's (SCSU) master's (MBA) program. Southern is in New Haven, not very far from Yale. I really wanted to go to Yale—I applied but did not even hear back. Also, I remember one of the professors laughed at my mention of attending Yale.

Not that a degree from Yale could validate me in any way, but I simply always wanted to push myself and prove that I could do what many deemed undoable.

In any case, I found a home at SCSU and finished the MBA in two years by taking a full load each semester including the summers and graduated cum laude (with honors). In under 4 years I finished a BS and an MBA, while working full-time and maintaining a family back in Egypt. I would fly back for the Christmas-winter break. The kids' summer vacation was spent with me and my mom in Waterbury. It was good for everybody, especially my mom. Summers in Waterbury became routine during those four years. Once I decided to enroll in a doctoral program, a roughly 5-year commitment, Layla and I decided to remain together in the US.

PhD Guidance: An Impromptu Meeting in Egypt

In the last semester of finishing up my master's degree during my annual Christmas-winter break trips to Egypt, my friend Omar met me at the airport as usual. Omar was a Blackamerican from the US, like me a Muslim revert who decided against raising his family in the US. He was one of the first Americans that I befriended when I first arrived in Egypt. O, as he came to be known, was my eyes and ears while I was in the US and he was always there for logistics like rides from the airport, rental cars, and anything else I needed prior to arrival and during my stay. O was from the Midwest and had been living in Egypt a few years prior to my initial arrival in 2003.

During my December 2012 trip to Egypt, O picked me up from the airport and told me that the Brother Muhammad Khalifa would also arrive the next day. And O said, "You two finally get to meet up." I already knew about Muhammad Khalifa because we had mutual friends, like O and some others. He also lived and studied in Egypt and our time there briefly overlapped. As I arrived in Egypt in 2003, Muhammad was returning to the US to get his doctorate degree. And by 2012, he was Dr. Khalifa, an assistant professor at Michigan State University (MSU).

This coincidental meeting in Egypt was timely and proved to contribute to another seismic shift in my life over the course of the next few years. Omar and I reconnected to pick up Dr. Khalifa from the airport the next day and Khalifa and I bonded almost instantly.

We had some passionate discussions and debates but it was clear that the brother was not just smart, but intellectually and historically grounded in traditions of Black knowledge. We challenged one another in critical and respectful ways. We met nearly every day over the course of two weeks that we were there. These daily interactions are what I would describe now as brotherhood and bonding.

I was finishing my master's degree and had already applied to several university doctoral programs. Several schools in North Carolina were at the top of the list, anywhere outside of Connecticut (I had been there for four plus years and it was time to go). I was telling Khalifa about doctoral degree plans and aspirations and he, knowing that I had worked in the school system in Egypt, encouraged me to consider a PhD in educational administration. He said, "Why don't you get your doctorate in educational administration?"

I had worked as an administrator in one of the private international K-12 school networks in Cairo. His suggestion made sense. Even though I had spent the last four years studying business administration, there was a lot of overlap and intersections with educational administration. He reasoned that I already had school administration and management experience, plus an understanding of logistics from owning and operating a business. His rationale helped me see the connections to educational administration, which was his discipline and field of study. A lightbulb went off.

Dr. Khalifa, did not promise me anything, but recommended that I apply to Michigan State, in the College of Education in the Department of K-12 Educational Administration. So I did. And ultimately I was accepted. I knew of Muhammad Khalifa for about nine years before we met in person in 2012 for the first time. What I learned about him over the years was that he epitomizes Black excellence and embodies the meaning of "each one, teach one." He put his reputation on the line for me.

Muhammad Khalifa, knowing about my background and what I had gone through must have sensed that I would honor his reputation. He mentored me through the application process and once I got accepted, I expressed my gratitude. His response was, ". . . when you get into this position, make sure you do the same thing for someone else. Help our people coming up to come up, because that's what the people before me did for me. That's how it's supposed to be." This was all the thanks and gratitude he wanted from me.

In that sense, telling this story and writing this book is part of Khalifa's sentiment—help bring or pull someone else up. Offer some clarity to those currently struggling in the ways that I struggled as a young boy and man. Help them to not lose hope or give up. I found myself grappling with wanting to stay far away from my past; I didn't care to revisit it and wished to detach myself from the trauma of the prison years and the losses of loved ones. I didn't want to live with the embarrassment of incarceration and having sold drugs in my youth. I didn't want to have to be conscious of that. But I know there are many young Black boys and young men across the US just like me. And my stories, failures, and triumphs are much bigger than me. They are lessons for my children and other generations of Black boys growing up and navigating life in the US from communities similar to mine. My biggest goal for this book is to teach, inspire, and mentor as many young minds from the pages of this book so that they can see the evolutionary/revolutionary possibilities in themselves.

From HBCU To MSU: Finishing What I Started

Although the master's degree (MBA) was a challenge and required a great deal of focus and discipline to finish, the PhD was incredibly more challenging. However, these were much more welcomed challenges than what I had grown accustomed. Upon starting the PhD I had to relocate my entire family from Egypt in the summer of 2013 to Connecticut and then eventually to Michigan for the start of the fall semester in August 2013.

This was a grueling transition at the start of a rigorous graduate program. Besides my own education, I had to enroll my sons in school, find suitable housing (which thankfully MSU provided a viable option for graduate students and visiting professors with families). The weather challenges for Layla and the kids and their first experiences with snow were memorable. The K-12 schools offered another kind of challenge for my boys—US-style institutional racism.

Anti-Blackness and racism in US schools is deeply systemic, well refined, and at times difficult to identify, and easily overlooked. My kids' experiences with racism in US schools included surveillance, placing my son in the front of the class to monitor his movements because as my son's fourth-grade teacher told me, "Your son was too social." I asked the teacher to tell me of a better quality than being able to connect and interact with different people? Of course he couldn't because it wasn't about that at all. I recall challenging my oldest son's fourth-grade teacher, an older white self-described civil rights advocate who pointed to the picture of Martin Luther King Jr. on his wall as proof that he was an antiracist, social justice educator. Despite the fact that all of his practices and interactions with my impressionable 9-year-old son were restrictive and controlling, all of which discouraged his academic confidence.

Although in Egypt we experienced a great deal of anti-Black prejudice, it was much different than US racism. Egyptian students mocked and bullied my kids' brown skin but their teachers believed in them, expected academic excellence, encouraged them, and validated their

153

intelligence. As a result, my kids responded and excelled academically in one of the most challenging private schools in the greater Cairo area. Yet back in the US, my kids' teachers made them question themselves and their intelligence, which caused measurable stagnation.

The rigors of a PhD program, and helping my sons navigate the same deficit academic norms I endured as a K-12 student, was exhausting. These challenges took a toll on our family and things began unravelling. Classes and my research assistant job in the department at MSU—were overwhelming. Given that it was Layla's first time being away from home, and the PhD program expectations placed on me nearly fractured our relationship beyond repair.

Silver Lining in the Turmoil

One of my most memorable experiences as a graduate student at MSU was at the end of my second year in 2015. I was granted a university-sponsored fellowship trip to Cuba. The trip was part of an international exchange between fifteen doctoral students and three faculty members, to learn firsthand from Cubans about their educational advances over the past several decades. This two-week fellowship took us across the island to Cienfuegos, Trinidad, and eventually Havana. We visited several K-12 schools and Cuban universities such as Cienfuegos, University of Havana, as well as one of their top medical schools Latin American School of Medicine (ELAM). We were greeted and informed about the island from a wide variety of people from educators, government officials, artists, musicians and every day Cubans.

Hearing from Cubans living in Cuba about their experiences was enlightening. We encountered a variety of perspectives some very candid and others measured. For example we heard from Afro-Cubans about the types of discrimination that they faced, and they told us that their skin color was a barrier. We also noticed with our own eyes that Afro-Cubans held many of the most menial and demeaning jobs. Our observations led to a discussion about anti-Black discrimination with educators at the University of Cienfuegos, which made our hosts anxious and defensive. They stressed that Cuba was not like the US and was a melting pot (*Mestizaje*) where discrimination based on color did not occur. This trip was unprecedented given that nearly half of the group of doctoral students were Blackamericans, whose research focused on Blackness and race in education. In addition one of the three faculty members was Dr. Muhammad Khalifa.

After Cienfuegos, it seemed that whomever we spoke with, other university or governments officials were very direct with us in matters of Blackness in Cuba and many even offered some crucial insights and history. For example, they explained to us how the US embassy rarely extended visas to Afro-Cubans, noting how they were not broadly represented abroad in the US and elsewhere. This unofficial practice, or non-practice of offering visas to Afro-Cubans, it was explained to us, carried significant ripple effects. For example, Cubans living abroad sent money back into the island, which provided a lever of support for their families and loved ones.

155

The unintended consequences of these practices allowed for, in some instances, families of fairer-skinned Cubans to help families build businesses, which contributed to a socioeconomic divide between Black and white Cubans. A divide which some argue did not exist during the revolution years. Another important insight revealed to us by Cubans was that after the revolution, the tourism industry was mostly run by whites from the US who refused to hire Black Cubans (1950s–1960s). As a result, one of the most, if not the most lucrative industries at that time excluded Afro-Cubans. These are just two insightful perspectives from the mouths of Cubans on the island; albeit Cuba's sociopolitics are far more involved than these discussions revealed. Furthermore, without oversimplifying the complexities of racism and anti-Blackness in Cuba, we found these perspectives insightful. Cuba was yet another one of my engagements with Blacks in the diaspora experiencing common anti-Black sentiments, although structured, practiced, and differed in intensity than what we experience in the US.

The *Value* of Black Men in Academia

Leading up to my graduation, I was frustrated with my program. The only two Black men in the department, who had mentored me and helped me navigate a hostile anti-Black climate at MSU, were both gone. Drs. Chris Dunbar and Muhammad Khalifa both departed for other universities. Yet both revealed that they did not want to leave MSU. And in my opinion, MSU's Department of K-12 Administration let their two most important faculty leave. I spent two critical years with them, which meant I had, at least, two more years left without my main sources of support and kinship. My time during the summer of 2015 in Cuba was my last interaction with Khalifa as an MSU faculty. Due to the lack of support I received after Drs. Dunbar and Khalifa left, I am certain that there was a strong sentiment that I could and would not finish.

Although I had lost a formidable and irreplaceable support network, I was able to complete my degree. Thanks to an unlikely supporter from outside of my department. Because of the clearly different treatment that I experienced after Drs. Dunbar and Khalifa departed, I considered boycotting the graduation ceremony for a simple graduation dinner with my mom and visiting family and friends. However, Dr. Lynn Fendler, who stepped up and into the director's role for my dissertation, helped me rethink boycotting graduation. She reminded me of how hard I had worked and how proud my family would be to share that moment. She was right. I decided to attend the university graduation ceremony at MSU's Breslin Center. I was able to locate my family and see my kids and mom beaming with pride and I realized how wrong I was for thinking about missing this event. This was not about me it was about them. All of the hardship and worries I put my mom through, this was the ultimate proof that I may have lived up to her most lofty expectations when just a few years prior it seemed impossible. A photo of me was captured on the jumbotron at the Breslin as I was receiving my degree. That jumbotron photo eventually ended up on a tee-shirt that family members had printed out and wore at a graduation party held for me in Waterbury months later.

More importantly, my mom was still not out of the woods with her battle with pancreatic cancer. Granted at this point, she was two years removed from surgery and in remission, but there had been signs that the cancer had returned. Making her proud made me proud. In hindsight, all of the growing pains that my kids experienced in Michigan and my challenges there were good for us. We built some great relationships in Michigan while at MSU and we eventually all left with fond memories. I had accepted a job as a professor in California, at San Diego State University (SDSU).

Southern California: Reflecting on the Past in the Future

My new professor job presented another steep challenge. I now have a responsibility to the people who believed in me, who went to bat for me, and those who picked me up and dusted me off after all the times I fell on my face. I have a responsibility to my mom for all that she sacrificed. I owe it to my kids to help them understand who their father was before and who he became later. Then there are the other young Black boys trying to understand and navigate life in the US where they are written off. My message to them: you can succeed and overcome; and remain your true self. Although I overcame a lot, it was not without precedent. Through the pages of a book I learned about Malcolm X, aka Al-Hajj Malik Shabazz, the best example of a street kid's transformation. Would he had ever turned to the streets if his K-12 educators believed in his intelligence and supported his goal to become a lawyer? His teachers sullied his aspirations of becoming a lawyer and instead recommended that he consider working with his hands.

158

This school culture of dissuading young Black brilliant minds from reaching their highest potential remains pervasive and prevalent today. The human evolution of Malcolm X is almost mythical; like a tale of David and Goliath. Black men are like David standing up to the Goliath that is the US. And for every one of us that have overcome the omnipotent Goliath there are far more casualties that go unnamed. These names include my childhood friends and heroes like Melle B., Ragar, C-Love, my father Butch Minor, my Cousin Tra Mack, and Sonnet from VSU. As a professor now, all of my hardships and life lessons travelled with me to Southern California and are now part of my worldview, my pedagogy and teaching strategies.

CHAPTER ELEVEN
The Setting of a Native Son

After five brutal winters in Michigan, I had the opportunity to move to one of the most beautiful cities on earth—San Diego. I write this book currently as an assistant professor at San Diego State University, in the college of education's department of educational leadership. My life's journey and what I had to overcome to get here is the result of faith. A collective of prayers from ancestors, elders, peers, and myself. The moment I entered prison at age 22, I began planning for this moment. Although I did not think it would take four years to get out, I knew I would overcome and redeem myself. Once I was released and started my music journey, incredible talent and resources became available in a short amount of time before I pulled the plug. Similarly, when I relocated to Egypt, doors opened that I could not have fathomed. And upon my return to the US, my educational journey, degrees, and the faculty position, were indeed the result of hard work and faith. Granted, the obstacles were tremendous; but it was faith, belief in myself but belief in a higher power greater than myself and the circumstances that I inherited.

Regardless of your beliefs we all live by faith. Some of us are more cognizant than others but faith encompasses all that we do. For example, if you have your day or week planned out, a trip planned months in advance, you are acting on faith in something bigger than you and beyond your control. You have placed faith in the sunrise in the morning that will light your path to go about your day. And in the sun setting in the evening, to allow your body the requisite rest needed for the day's activities that that you planned. Even more so, you have faith that you will wake up in the morning, an act outside of your control, and faith that you will live long enough to go on that vacation that you planned and paid for. However, the reality is that none of these things, as much as we take them for granted, are in our control. We have no control of the sun setting and rising, and no control of when, where, and how we will die.

Sunshine in the Reign of White Supremacy

This is not a book to satisfy those obsessed with ideas of meritocracy nor is it necessarily prescriptive. My ability to attain a doctorate degree after tremendous downfalls and obstacles is not meant to be an olive branch to white supremacy. In other words, my goal is not for this book to be paraded around as evidence that hard work and pulling up boot straps are the solutions to white supremacy systems, norms, and practices. Much of what I had to overcome and battle through are directly related to a long historical tradition of white supremacy based oppression and obstacles.

Furthermore, Black kids, particularly in the US, who find themselves growing up in environments similar to mine, or who are engulfed by similar traps can know there are still ways out. But at the same time what Blacks in the US are forced to endure and overcome is unjust.

Both are true: white supremacy is suffocating our communities and there are ways out.

There are those of us navigating drug infested, economically and politically divested communities where police act more as an occupying deadly force than protectors and servants. Where schools do not educate students in a manner that reflects their experiences or even their interests, and are misaligned from their culture and customs. Additionally, these deficit educational practices are exacerbated by white educators miseducating Black students, through indifference or disdain for Black people and culture. And the fact that white educators who have been openly hostile toward Black children and our communities are allowed to enter schools where Black students go to learn is another indication of the type of violence Blacks are asked to endure and remain silent about.

The current imbalance of loving, caring, and understanding Black educators educating Black students is a major contributor to the phenomenon of unmotivated Black students, many of whom are bright and highly intelligent. Contemporary schooling processes have routinely miseducated generations of Black children, and helped stagnate Black communities. My advanced degrees had a purpose beyond showing my family, community, and doubters that I could surpass external limitations. My purpose was also to take part in highlighting these problems with schools and Black students as just mentioned; and contribute to sustainable, systemic change. But even more so, amplify the call for Black education led by loving and caring Black educators.

162

Academia is the whitest place I have ever experienced, and it is cold and unwelcoming. The world that had nurtured me and that I had grown used to was different from this strange new world that I had chosen to integrate. I am more comfortable living near and off the grid of societal expectations. Especially default Eurocentric expectations.

This is America . . . But So Is *That*

January 6, 2021 offered the rest of the world what Blacks in the US already knew. There are separate applications of law and standards in the US. Black protestors literally attacking the government in search of government officials to inflict harm on them would have ended with a blood bath. However, the extremely careful, thoughtful, and considerate engagement with January 6 insurrectionists/protestors, depending on who you ask, placed the racial division in the US on a global platform and under a microscope. The heavy-handed response to protests related to unlawful and unjust deaths of Blacks—especially when juxtaposed with January 6th—is remarkable and does not need much commentary. Blacks in the US unfortunately are inherently aware of US double standards. This awareness is inherited and experienced as commonly as breathing.

My academic trajectory, my new position and my colleagues and peers forced me to reanalyze the Black underground where so many Black people feel most comfortable. Although far from perfect, it is deeply rooted in culture and tradition; replete with codes of ethics, communication, a sense of community, brotherhood, and family. There are plenty of exceptions, shortcomings, a fair share of hardships and injustices that are both external and internal. Yet overall there is a sense of belonging. It is an unmistakable energy that is embraced by those who recognize and find it comforting. Also in these underground/off-the-grid communities exists an economy, not all of which is deemed *legal* or *ethical* by our establishment—the same one that necessitated it. Nonetheless, it is creative, ingenious, born out of struggle, and a form of resistance to historical white economic violence and imposition.

Diamonds: The Pressures of a Rough Small Town

I have travelled the world and I have come to believe, which is no secret to Waterburians. Pound for pound, Waterbury produces some of the most talented and untapped talent anywhere. Creatives, entrepreneurs, and hustlers of all kinds; working-class people many who can't afford to move, and others who are content. And many more who long migrated and are thriving elsewhere in various adopted states and cities.

Beginning in November of 2018 when I lost my Cousin Tra Mack and then six months later, my mom, I lost two of the most influential people in my life. My mom nurtured me and was a constant source of wisdom and understanding in my life; always there throughout years of arrests, fights, sleepless nights, and no matter what, she always offered me a place to lay my head and food to eat. However, she never coddled me, she didn't tolerate my nonsense, and when I was wrong she called me out: Tough love personified.

As for Tra Mack, he remains my first hero. For as long as I could remember I looked up to and wanted to be like my most extraordinary first cousin. His maturity made him seem much older than he was when we were younger. We all seemed to huddle around him and he was the glue that kept all of us together. Although he spent many years in prison and never finished high school, he was easily one of the smartest and most talented people in my family and one of the most beloved, not just in my family but by so many throughout Waterbury.

In the early 1990s, my Cousin Tra Mack was shot in his back by Waterbury police officers (WPD). Tra was in his early to mid-20s and unarmed at the time of the shooting. The bullet entered his lower back and traveled enough to ruin his reproductive organs. Tra didn't have any kids then, and as a result of the shooting he never had any. Back then, it was rare for WPD to shoot at any of us. Now, however, it seems as if there has been a marked shift in police shootings of unarmed Black men nation-wide. My Cousin Tra Mack was the first such instance of a police shooting in our area that I can recall, which made it a high-profile case.

WPD did tons of other foul shit like harass, beat up, and plant drugs on innocent Black and Brown people for no reason, and steal their money. But unprovoked shootings was a new low. On the heels of the Rodney King verdict, the shooting of my Cousin Tra Mack sparked huge outcry. Tra filed a high-profile lawsuit against WPD. The lawsuit was countered by round-the-clock surveillance of my grandmother's house, where Tra Mack spent a lot of his time. In his younger years, Tra dabbled in drug use, but I think the shooting led to a heroin addiction. The round-the-clock surveillance and his heroin habit led to him being arrested nearly every time he left the house. The local news media framed my cousin as a menace to society who deserved to be shot in the back. The surveillance, subsequent arrests, and news coverage led to a dismissal of Tra's lawsuit and a conviction, which led to nine years incarcerated.

More than a Wedding: A Reunion, Last Goodbyes, and Deep Reflections

My Cousin Baron's wedding marked my first time in CT after completing my doctorate. On October 19, 2018, the night before the wedding Cousin Tra Mack, now fighting for his life battling cancer, and I stayed up all night talking, reminiscing, and reflecting. Those conversations exposed deep roots and a pride to have grown up in our family. I left CT fully aware and content that I probably saw my cousin for the last time. I was right. He died on November 12, 2018.

On May 30, 2019, my mother died as I was still grieving Tra Mack. I still do not have the words that describe this compilation of pain and those months afterwards. Even though mom had been sick for four years, nothing could have prepared me for losing her. I miss her subtle and not-so-subtle ways of correcting me; even her overstepping her boundaries to advise me on marriage or parenting missteps. We had our share of clashes over time. Yet iron sharpens iron, and who I am today reflects her tough but loving and nurturing way.

Epilogue

The trauma of my life's experiences (prison, streets, interactions with police) is laid bare in this book. Accordingly, I come to the world of academia through a different path. A path that has always been the subject of academic inquiry where insiders (like me and members from communities in Waterbury where I was raised) rarely participate. I naively entered the academy excited and expecting to be seen as a missing piece of their puzzle. Since so much research is conducted on individuals such as me and communities like mine, e.g., school-to-prison pipeline, failing minority-majority schools, culturally disconnected white teachers in urban and inner-city schools, children from communities with high rates of poverty and crime, I thought I would be recognized and warmly received. However, that was not the case. I learned quickly that in academia, as part of public policy discourse, the stated goals have multiple meanings depending on factors such as race, socioeconomic and political status. Nonetheless, academia gave me the most intimate look into the US power grid. These insights provided a new understanding of how and why US public policy continues to fail Blacks miserably despite trillions of dollars in spending and decades of policy and legislation *reforms*.

Also, as currently set up, the academy isn't designed for mutual understanding. The (white) patriarchal and authoritative *all-knowing* men manning the ivory tower are not interested in understanding, only to be understood. For example, as a professor in education, my colleagues and I work toward similar goals around better serving Black and other similarly minoritized students. However, white men design, drive, and oversee these efforts. Eurocentric ideologies and canons govern the strategies, theories, curriculum, and contrived best-practices.

Similarly, white men and their canons govern the reforms and oversee the matrix of grant funding, training, and hiring educators responsible for educating Black students in schools. Even when none of the students are white or when all of them are Black. I have had over a decade of interactions with these knowledge production institutions and organizations and their interworking to know firsthand.

Pulling the Past into the Present

I started this book outlining my family's migration from the South, a historical moment known as the Great Migration—the documentation of millions of Blacks fleeing the terror and horrors of Jim Crow for faraway lands a few decades post-enslavement. The circumstances, hopes, and dreams of Black migrants fleeing Jim Crow are no different than those who migrated to the US fleeing violence or hardships found back home. As a result, there is much for migrant communities, especially Blacks from across the diaspora, to learn about the Great Blackamerican migration within the US—a valuable, much overlooked, and misunderstood component of migrant studies and US history. The ways in which US history is taught in schools, at best, gloss over its fundamentally violent past; and, at worst,

168

ignore and rewrite it. Accordingly, perspectives that contradict Eurocentrism and highlight the historical violence from which US power emerged are marginalized and prevented mainstream access.

Accordingly, education that doesn't include alternative perspectives, even contrarian and adversarial ones, fails to teach the full human experience and loses credibility. Furthermore, society suffers, and a critically informed future becomes jeopardized. History will not reflect favorably on the consecutive decades of educational practices since the Supreme Court disbanded segregated schools. Blacks in the US continue to have our fundamental human rights denied and our dignity trampled by public policy and political leaders, irrespective of party and affiliation. We must not expect any alternative pathways until a meaningful change is demanded. A serious look at US history offers little indication of benevolent white people changing the course laid by their ancestors without a *demand*. Frederick Douglass warned us of this in 1857.

My journey led me to understand that education must include exposure to genocide, enslavement, breaking of treaties, and the economic systems built from these horrors; and the families, organizations, and individuals whose political and economic positions today are its heirs. Tell it all and then repair the harm. Until then, we will continue perpetuating violent lies and myths sold to the world about the US. These are my stories and my interpretations of the *truth*. I do not speak for all Blackamericans, and I don't pretend we are a monolith. However, what is monolithic about us is our engagement with white supremacy and how it imposes upon every facet of our existence and affairs. My testimony is intended to offer hope, clarity, and motivation to young Black boys and men throughout the diaspora, their families, and others who love and are concerned for them.

The Diaspora: United in Blackness Divided by Whiteness

Blackamericans are unfairly measured by the experiences of other Black people throughout the diaspora, where consequently, Black people control the political and school systems—and at the bare minimum, the educators look like them. Blackamericans have had control commandeered away and have been systemically prevented from controlling the most meaningful systems, especially those related to educating their children. This imposition results partly from constant, covert, and overt factual and proven conspiracies. If this seems farfetched, learn about the Wilmington coup and massacre in North Carolina 1898 and the destruction of Black Wall Street and the massacre in Tulsa, Oklahoma in 1921. Revisit or get familiar with COINTELPRO, what this secret government program did and how it operated at its peak in the 1960s—the Black leaders it spied on and targeted for assassination. The organizations it infiltrated and destroyed from within covertly.

Under COINTELPRO, resistance to Black progress became a national priority, funded with resources allocated by the US government, covertly approved by US Presidents, and executed at the highest levels of law enforcement in the name of national security. Or learn about the Supreme Court's *Brown v. Board of Education* decision to end segregated schools and the resultant loss of jobs for over 100,000 qualified, excellent, highly credentialed, and educated Black educators—school leaders and teachers.

And *The Hearings Before the Select Committee on Equal Educational Opportunity of the United States*, 92nd Congress, first session on equal educational opportunity in San Francisco, 1971, which were held in response to the elimination of a 100-year-old Black educational system and network. This is by no means an exhaustive list, yet each example, on its own, should be the subject of serious inquiry, investigation, and reparations.

This continuous stream of opposition to Black progress in the US is blatantly apparent and equally abhorrent in each generation of US history with no skips. I lived through the crack era and the mass incarceration epidemic in the 1990s, which needs to be part of a deep analysis juxtaposed with COINTELPRO and placed into context with US history relative to the Blackamerican experience in the US.

About the Author

James Wright is an assistant professor in the Department of Educational Leadership at San Diego State University. His research critically analyzes the various ways in which race and culture shape educational policy. Specifically, he looks at contemporary educational practices, informed by school policies, as impacted by historically racialized inequities that have become school norms.

Made in the USA
Las Vegas, NV
07 March 2023

68686197R00111